Series 6 Investment Company and Variable Contracts Products Representative Qualification Exam Practice Questions & Dumps

Exam Practice Questions for Finra Series 6
LATEST VERSION

Presented By: Quantic Books

Quantic
Books

Copyright © 2020 by Quantic Books
All rights reserved. No part of this publication may be recreated, kept in reclamation system, or sent out, in any way or by any methods, electronic, mechanical, duplicating, recording or otherwise, without the prior consent of the copyright owner.
First Copy Printed in 2020

About Quantic Books:

Quantic Books is a publishing house based in Princeton, New Jersey, USA. , a platform that is accessible online as well as locally, which gives power to educational content, erudite collection, poetry & many other book genres. We make it easy for writers & authors to get their books designed, published, promoted, and sell professionally on worldwide scale with eBook + Print distribution. Quantic Books is now distributing books worldwide.

Note: Find answers of the questions at the last of the book.

QUESTION 1

The Uniform Securities Act (USA) is

A. a body of laws governing the purchase and sale of securities within a single state.
B. a set of guidelines for individual states to follow when formulating their own securities' laws.
C. a group of laws requiring state-issued securities, such as municipal bonds, to be registered with.
D. federal legislation that requires all states to adopt the same registration requirements for all.

QUESTION 2

Once you have passed the Series 63 examination, which entity must then approve your application to sell securities?

A. FINRA
B. NASAA
C. SEC
D. the state administrator

QUESTION 3

Which of the following securities would not necessarily be exempt from state registration?

A. a stock listed on the Tokyo Stock Exchange
B. a bond guaranteed by the Canadian government
C. a bond issued by another state's employees' credit union
D. a stock listed as a NASDAQ National Market Issue.

QUESTION 4

Moe is a registered investment adviser doing business under the name of MoeMoney Investment Advisers, LLC. Larry, Curly, and Mary all hold positions with the firm. Larry is on the board of directors; Mary is a sales representative for the firm; and Curly is an administrative assistant, who performs clerical duties.

Given that Moe is already a registered investment adviser, which of the other three are automatically registered as investment adviser representatives?

A. Larry only
B. Larry and Mary only
C. Larry, Mary and Curly
D. Mary and Curly only

QUESTION 5

Jack is employed by NewCorp, which is engaging in an initial public offering (IPO). Jack will need to register as a sales representative if he:

A. engages in transactions with the underwriters of the IPO for the purpose of taking the firm public.
B. represents NewCorp in any transactions with financial institutions.
C. participates in the selling of the new stock to individual investors.
D. Jack will need to register as a sales representative if he performs any one of the above activities.

QUESTION 6

Blue Sky Laws are designed to:

A. protect investors from fraud in their securities market transactions.
B. protect agents, broker-dealers, and investment advisers and their representatives from spurious allegations of fraudulent activity.
C. enhance the tourism industry within a state.
D. favor investment in companies that engage in environmentally friendly practices.

QUESTION 7

An individual who represents a broker-dealer in the buying and selling of securities is called a(n):

A. underwriter
B. issuer
C. agent
D. administrator

QUESTION 8

Which of the following statements best explains the difference between an agent and a broker-dealer?

A. An agent is an individual who represents a broker-dealer or an issuer and buys and sells securities he does not own in return for a commission on the transactions he executes. A broker-dealer may also buy and sell securities for his own portfolio, in which case the broker-dealer enjoys any price appreciation on those securities.
B. A broker-dealer must be licensed in the state in which he conducts business, but there are no separate licensing requirements for agents.
C. Agents are engaged exclusively in the purchase and sale of stocks whereas broker-dealers also buy and sell bonds and option contracts.
D. Agents conduct their business exclusively in the secondary market, while broker-dealers also operate in the primary market.

QUESTION 9

Rich Writewell wants to begin publishing an independent weekly financial newsletter that will provide investment recommendations as well as other financial news items to the general public. Rich hopes that his newsletter will achieve nationwide circulation within a few months.
Which of the following statements is true?

A. Rich will have to register as an investment adviser since his publication will include investment recommendations.
B. Rich will have to register as an investment adviser only if he sells this newsletter to the public. If the publication is to be distributed free of charge, he will not have to register.
C. Rich may be exempt from registering as an investment adviser if he is a lawyer, accountant, engineer, or teacher. Otherwise, he will have to register.
D. Rich will not have to register as an investment adviser since he is publishing a legitimate financial newsletter for distribution to the general public.

QUESTION 10

Erin is a registered agent who works for SecureMoney Brokers-dealers. One of her clients, Mrs. McTurk, is a recently-widowed woman who relies on Erin for advice about her investment portfolio. Mrs. McTurk reminds Erin of her own grandmother, and she is happy to provide guidance within the sphere of her own knowledge.

Based on these facts, which of the following statements is true?

A. SecureMoney Broker-dealers must register as an investment adviser since one of its employees is providing investment advice.
B. Erin must register as an investment adviser since she is providing investment advice.
C. SecureMoney Broker-dealers must register as an investment adviser since one of its employees is providing investment advice, and Erin must register as an investment adviser representative as the firm's employee.
D. Neither SecureMoney Broker-dealers nor Erin must register as an investment adviser based on the facts provided.

QUESTION 11

Which of the following would not fall under the classification of "institutional investor"?

A. Prudential Insurance
B. Chase Bank
C. Neuring Investment Advisers
D. Franklin Templeton Mutual Funds

QUESTION 12

Which of the following is an example of a non-issuer transaction?

A. IBM sells a new issue of bonds to an insurance company.
B. Jose purchases a 10-year bond issued by Progress Energy when it has 6 years remaining to maturity.
C. Google offers more shares of its stock for sale to the public.
D. NewCorp, which has been a privately held company, is engaging in an initial public offering (IPO) of its stock.

QUESTION 13

Which of the following is not considered to be a security, as defined by the Uniform Securities Act (USA)?

A. a debenture
B. a certificate of deposit (CD)
C. a put option
D. an annuity contract wherein an insurance company promises to pay a fixed sum, either in a lump amount or through periodic payments.

QUESTION 14

Which of the following scenarios would not be considered a "sale," as defined by the Uniform Securities Act (USA)?

I. Yoshito owned shares of Minnow Corporation and received shares of Whale Corporation from Whale when it merged with Minnow.
II. Olivia's uncle, an agent with SecureMoney Brokers, sold Olivia ten call options on the stock of Microsoft.
III. Hans purchased a bond of Indebted Corporation that had detachable warrants and subsequently sold the warrants.
IV. Tom pledged some shares of stock he owned personally to secure a business loan for his company.

A. Neither I nor II would be considered sales.
B. Neither II nor III would be considered sales.
C. Neither I nor IV would be considered sales.
D. Neither III nor IV would be considered sales.

QUESTION 15

Jeremy Sly considered himself somewhat of an inventor. The only problem was that his day job interfered with his opportunity to exercise his creativity. He came up with a plan to get outside investors to support his inventive activities. To this end, he produced and distributed a brochure advertising partnership interests with a guaranteed return on investment of at least 15% after the first 12 months, based on what he had allegedly generated from his other (non-existent) inventions.

Given these facts, is Jeremy guilty of any security violations under the Uniform Securities Act (USA)?

A. No. The facts don't indicate whether any partnership interests were actually sold, and there can be no violation unless there is a sale.
B. No. An interest in a partnership is not considered a security.
C. No. It is not against the law to believe in oneself and promote one's ideas.
D. Yes. Even an "offer" to sell securities must not contain any untruths.

QUESTION 16

Although an Administrator has broad powers, he or she cannot:

A. issue subpoenas involving compulsory attendance.
B. gather evidence.
C. deliver a judicial injunction.
D. formulate rules and orders.

QUESTION 17

"Federal covered securities" were defined and exempted from state registration requirements by the:

A. National Securities Markets Improvement Act of 1996 (NSMIA.)
B. Gramm-Leach-Bliley Act of 1999 (GLBA.)
C. Uniform Securities Act (USA.)
D. National Conference of Commissioners on Uniform State Laws (NCCUSL.)

QUESTION 18

Rich Quick is a broker-dealer licensed in the state of Massachusetts and has offices only within the state. Two of Rich Quick's clients regularly vacation in Florida during the winter months, and Rich Quick executes trades for them when they call him from out-of-state.

Based on these facts,

I. Rich Quick needs to register as a broker-dealer in the state of Florida as well.
II. Rich Quick needs to register only as an agent in the state of Florida.
III. Rich Quick needs to establish an office in the state of Florida in order to transact business.
IV. Rich Quick need not register in Florida.

A. Statements I and III are true.
B. Statements II and III are true.
C. Only Statement I is true.
D. Only Statement IV is true.

QUESTION 19

Most individual state securities laws today are based on:

A. the Uniform Securities Act of 1956.
B. the Uniform Securities Act of 2002.
C. the National Securities Markets Improvement Act of 1996.
D. the Gramm-Leach-Bliley Act of 1999.

QUESTION 20

BigCash Broker-Dealers is registered in the state and is in the process of purchasing a smaller broker-dealer, Target Investments, as a subsidiary. Target Investments is also registered in the state.

After completing the purchase, what actions must BigCash take regarding registration of its new subsidiary?

A. BigCash need do nothing since Target Investments was already duly registered with the state as a broker-dealer.
B. BigCash must file a new application with the state to register its new subsidiary, but will be able to utilize the remainder of any annual filing fees that Target Investments had paid for the year.
C. BigCash must file a new application with the state to register its new subsidiary and must also pay the annual filing fees required by the Administrator.
D. BigCash will need to pay the annual filing fees required by the Administrator, but will not need to file a new registration application.

QUESTION 21

In order to maintain its registration with a state, a broker-dealer may be required to:

I. take a written or oral exam.
II. pay an annual filing fee.
III. maintain a minimum net capital.
IV. file all advertising material with the Administrator.

A. I and II only
B. II and III only
C. II, III, and IV only
D. I, II, III, and IV

QUESTION 22

Once a broker-dealer has applied for and been granted state registration, the registration remains valid

A. until December 31st.
B. for twelve months.
C. for three years.
D. for five years.

QUESTION 23

A broker-dealer is required to keep his records for how long?

A. at least three years
B. at least five years
C. at least seven years
D. broker-dealer is required to keep his records for as long as he is registered in the state.

QUESTION 24

Which of the following entities would be required to register with the state as a broker-dealer under the guidelines of the Uniform Securities Act (USA)?

A. an underwriter with no offices in the state that is helping a firm that is incorporated within the state with the sale of its new bond issue to insurance companies.
B. a credit union that operates within the state and provides loans to its members.
C. an agent who executes the purchase and sale of stocks and bonds for his clients.
D. None of the above entities would be required to register with the state as a broker-dealer under the guidelines of the Uniform Securities Act.

QUESTION 25

Joe Romeo is a broker-dealer registered with the state. He has recently hired Betty Buxom as his administrative assistant. As part of her duties, he has given her the responsibility for effecting the purchases and sales of securities for some of his firm's smaller accounts. Ms. Buxom has never applied for nor been granted registration as a broker-dealer or agent. Based on these facts,

A. the Administrator is required by the Uniform Securities Act to revoke Joe Romeo's registration and file criminal and civil charges against him.
B. there is no problem as long as Ms. Buxom registers with the state as an agent within thirty days.
C. the Administrator may elect to revoke or suspend Joe Romeo's registration, and Joe may also face both civil and criminal penalties.
D. the Administrator is required to turn the case over to the state's district attorney, who will file criminal charges against both Joe Romeo and Betty Buxom.

QUESTION 26

Until yesterday Maddie was a registered agent employed by the broker-dealer, QuikDeals. Yesterday afternoon, issues that had been brewing between her and another employee of the firm came to a head, and Maddie impulsively quit her job.

At this point,

A. Maddie has thirty days to find a job with another broker-dealer, or she will need to file a new registration application.
B. Maddie has sixty days to find a job with another broker-dealer, or she will need to file a new registration application.
C. Maddie will have to file a new application for registration with the Administrator upon finding employment with another broker-dealer since she is no longer considered to be a registered agent by the state.
D. Maddie is required to call all of her clients at QuikDeals to inform them she is no longer employed there.

QUESTION 27

Maddie, a registered agent affiliated with broker-dealer QuikDeals, quit her job on the spur of the moment. Under the guidelines of the Uniform Securities Act (USA), who is responsible for notifying the Administrator?

A. QuikDeals has the sole responsibility for notifying the Administrator. Maddie is no longer deemed to be an agent after she terminated her relationship with QuikDeals, so she need do nothing.
B. Maddie has the sole responsibility for notifying the Administrator.
C. It depends. If Maddie becomes affiliated with another broker-dealer within thirty days, then she must notify the Administrator of her termination with QuikDeals and her current affiliation with the new firm. Otherwise, only QuikDeals must notify the Administrator.
D. Both QuikDeals and Maddie are responsible for notifying the Administrator.

QUESTION 28

Trevor is currently a registered agent in the state of Connecticut where he has been employed by Connect & Company, a broker-dealer that is registered in Connecticut and has subsidiary operations in Massachusetts, New Jersey, and New York. Trevor has moved to Massachusetts and is now associated with one of Connect's subsidiaries, a broker-dealer registered in the state. Trevor has applied to the Administrator of Massachusetts for registration as an agent.
Can Trevor execute purchases and sales for clients while his registration is still pending?

A. No. Until he is informed by the Administrator of Massachusetts that his application has been accepted, Trevor may not affect any securities transactions in Massachusetts.
B. Yes. Because Trevor is a registered agent in another state and is affiliated with a broker-dealer that is registered in the state of Massachusetts, he is not restricted from executing trades.
C. Yes. Trevor can execute trades for new clients he solicits, but only for sixty days while his registration is pending.
D. It depends. Trevor can execute some purchases and sales, but only for clients that he already had who may have recently relocated to Massachusetts and only for sixty days while his registration is pending.

QUESTION 29

Ms. Ding is an administrative assistant to the manager of a mutual fund. Most of her day is spent entering data onto a spreadsheet for her boss and answering phone calls. Some of the calls require her to provide information about the some of the fund's financial aspects, such as its closing net asset value on the previous day.

What type of registration does Ms. Ding require in order to perform her duties?

A. Ms. Ding needs to apply for registration as an agent since she is providing financial information.
B. Ms. Ding needs to apply for registration as an investment adviser representative since she is providing information about a specific mutual fund.
C. Ms. Ding will need to apply for registration as both an agent and an investment adviser representative in this case since she is providing information about a mutual fund.
D. Ms. Ding does not need to apply for any type of registration. She is merely supplying information and is not engaged in the purchase or sale of the fund shares.

QUESTION 30

Which of the following statements about agents is (are) false?

A. If an agent files for bankruptcy, the Administrator may elect to terminate that agent's registration if the Administrator believes it is "in the public interest" to do so.
B. When an agent has a change of address, both he and his broker-dealer affiliate must inform the Administrator.
C. An agent must demonstrate a specific minimum level of financial stability for his registration application to be accepted.
D. All of the above are false statements.

QUESTION 31

Which of the following entities must sign a "consent to service of process," thereby allowing the Administrator to receive legal documents that are meant to be served to the entity in place of that entity?

I. agents
II. investment advisers
III. investment adviser representatives
IV. broker-dealers

A. I and IV only
B. II and III only
C. II and IV only
D. I, II, III, and IV

QUESTION 32

Which of the following would fall under the definition of "agent," as defined by the Uniform Securities Act (USA)?

A. Joe works as an administrative assistant for broker-dealer GetErDone, doing data entry, filing client forms that contain confidential information, and directing calls to registered representatives of the firm.
B. Freedom broker-dealers executes the purchase and sale of securities for its customers.
C. TrustUs Bank has a subsidiary operation that sells mutual funds to the public.
D. None of the above would fall under the definition of "agent," as defined by the Uniform Securities Act (USA.)

QUESTION 33

The 2003 NASAA Model Rule requires that investment advisers that are not federal covered maintain their records for at least

A. three years.
B. five years.
C. seven years.
D. Investment advisers must maintain their records for as long as they remain registered with the state.

QUESTION 34

Individual states are prohibited from requiring a broker-dealer or investment adviser to file financial reports more frequently than:

A. once a year.
B. twice a year.
C. four times a year.
D. twelve times a year.

QUESTION 35

A-2-Z Associates advertises itself as a full service brokerage firm that will buy and sell securities for its clients, as well as provide investment advice to them. Its brochure provides a variety of plans to which a client can subscribe. The basic plan is the cheapest and allows the client a maximum number of trades per month for a specified fee. Another, slightly more expensive, plan provides the client with the same maximum number of trades per month, but the client also receives a personalized quarterly review of his portfolio along with advice for restructuring his portfolio based on such factors as current market conditions and specific industry or company information. The most expensive plan is one in which the client is assigned to an individual portfolio manager, who will take total responsibility for the asset allocation of the client's portfolio and will provide the client with monthly reports. Based on the services A-2-Z provides, it must register with the state as:

A. a broker-dealer.
B. an investment adviser.
C. both a broker-dealer and an investment adviser.
D. an investment adviser representative.

QUESTION 36

MoeMoney Investment Advisers, LLC is registered in the state of Texas, and its three offices are all located in the greater Dallas-Fort Worth area. Five of its clients- all individuals-have relocated to Colorado and all have indicated a desire to retain the services of MoeMoney. In order for this to be possible,

A. MoeMoney will need to apply for and be granted registration as an investment adviser in the state of Colorado.
B. each client will have to write a letter to the Administrator of the state of Colorado on MoeMoney's behalf.
C. MoeMoney will need to apply for and be granted registration as an investment adviser representative in the state of Colorado.
D. Neither MoeMoney nor its clients need do anything.

QUESTION 37

Sam Shade had his agent's license revoked by the state of Washington for repeatedly making misleading claims about various investment to investors. He had had it with all the rain anyway and decided to move to the sunshine state of Florida. His brother-in-law was a computer whiz who made money on the side (more than his day job provided, in fact) by supplying illegal immigrants with official-looking documentation, including social security numbers. Sam Shade became Ian Creed in a few clicks of the mouse. As Ian Creed, Sam was hired by Sunny Investment Advisers, an investment adviser firm located in the Florida Keys, in a clerical role. As such, Sam/Ian had access to the confidential information of the firm's clients, which he and his brother-in-law utilized for the purpose of identity theft. Under the Uniform Securities Act guidelines, when Sam and his brother-in-law are caught in their illegal activities,

A. Sunny Investment Advisers will not be held liable if it can prove that there was no way it could have or should have known of the revocation of Sam Shade's (aka Ian Creed) license.
B. Sunny Investment Advisers will be subject to criminal prosecution for employing an individual whose license had been revoked by the Administrator of another state since it obviously did not use due diligence in hiring Ian Creed, aka Sam Shade.
C. Sunny Investment Advisers will be subject to civil penalties for employing an individual whose license had been revoked by the Administrator of another state.
D. Sunny Investment Advisers will be subject to both criminal prosecution and civil penalties for employing an individual whose license had been revoked by the Administrator of another state since it obviously did not use due diligence in hiring Ian Creed, aka Sam Shade.

QUESTION 38

Which of the following statements regarding an investment adviser representative who has an office in the state is true?

A. If the investment adviser is registered with the SEC, then neither the investment adviser nor any of its affiliated investment adviser representative needs to be registered with the state.
B. Regardless of whether the investment adviser is registered with the SEC or is registered with the state, all investment adviser representatives of the firm must be registered with the state if they have offices in the state.
C. If the investment adviser that the investment adviser representative is affiliated with is itself registered with the state, then the investment adviser representative does not need to apply for a separate registration, regardless of whether the investment adviser representative has an office in the state.
D. If an investment adviser representative is registered with the SEC, he or she need not obtain state registration, regardless of whether the investment adviser representative has an office in the state.

QUESTION 39

A variable annuity is:

A. not a security and, therefore, does not have to be registered with the state.
B. not a security, but is still required to be registered with the state before it can be offered for sale.
C. a security and, therefore, has to be registered with the state before it can be offered for sale.
D. a security, but is exempt from state registration.

QUESTION 40

Which of the following is not a security, as defined by the Uniform Securities Act?

I. an option contract
II. a futures contract on gold
III. a 401K plan
IV. a variable annuity

A. None of the selections listed are securities.
B. Only Selection III is not a security.
C. Only Selections II and III are not securities.
D. Selections II, III and IV are not securities.

QUESTION 41

An arrangement wherein a terminally ill person sells a second party his life insurance policy at a discount from its face value, giving the buyer the right to the policy's face value when the seller dies is called a:

A. death warrant.
B. viatical settlement.
C. deceased option.
D. life straddle.

QUESTION 42

Mr. Bigwig, CEO of HiGrowth Corporation, meets with the president of BigFee Investment Bankers and arranges for BigFee to underwrite an Initial Public Offering (IPO) for the firm.

When the IPO comes to market, GetErDone Broker-Dealers is part of the selling group, which handles the sale of the stock to the public. In this scenario, which party is the issuer?

A. HiGrowth Corporation
B. Mr. Bigwig
C. BigFee Investment Bankers
D. GetErDone Broker-Dealers

QUESTION 43

Assuming the security is not registered under the Uniform Securities Act, which of the following would not be exempt from state registration?

A. a variable annuity contract offered by an insurance company with offices in the state
B. a stock that is listed on the American Stock Exchange
C. a stock that is listed on the OTC Bulletin Board
D. a put option on a stock that sells in the over-the-counter market

QUESTION 44

Under the Uniform Securities Act, which of the following does not need to be included when filing to register a security issue with the state?

A. a copy of the firm's articles of incorporation and bylaws, or the equivalent
B. copies of the underwriter agreements
C. a copy of any indenture applying to the security being registered
D. All of the above documents must be included when filing to register a security with the state.

QUESTION 45

For how long after the effective date is a security's registration valid?

A. three months
B. six months
C. one year
D. two years

QUESTION 46

A "notice filing" refers to

A. the right of an issuer to run tombstone ads in the newspapers and other publications upon filing a registration application with the state Administrator.
B. the filing by a federal covered investment adviser of forms already filed with the SEC along with a consent to service of process with the state Administrator.
C. a document that the issuer must file with the SEC informing the SEC that the firm has applied to the state for registration of its new security.
D. notification to the public by the issuer or its underwriters that the issue is being sold on an "all or nothing" basis.

QUESTION 47

Under the 2002 Uniform Securities Act, registration by coordination allows:

A. federal covered securities to be registered simultaneously with the SEC and with the states in which the securities will be offered for sale.
B. securities that do not fall within the category of federal covered securities to be registered simultaneously with the SEC and with the states in which the securities will be offered for sale.
C. both state-registered and out-of-state investment bankers to participate in the underwriting and registration of a new security issue.
D. issuers of federal covered securities to submit only a notice filing with the Administrator of states in which the securities will be offered for sale.

QUESTION 48

Newbie Corporation is considering the possibility of an interstate initial public offering (IPO) of its stock. In the initial meetings with BigFee Investment Bankers, Newbie has learned that the underwriting spread will be 15%. Although the actual offering price won't be set until Newbie's registration statement is approved by the SEC, BigFee has indicated that the offer price will probably be between $3 and $4 a share and that the stock will initially be listed on the OTC Bulletin Board.

What methods for state registration does Newbie have available?

I. registration by coordination
II. registration by notification
III. registration by qualification

A. Newbie may elect to register by any one of the above methods although registration by qualification would be the most burdensome choice.
B. Method I only
C. Methods I and III only
D. Method II only

QUESTION 49

Which of the following is not one of the criteria for a security to be eligible for registration by notification?

A. The issuer must have preferred stockholders as well as common stockholders.
B. The issuer must have a net worth of $4 million, or its net income before tax for at least two of the
C. The issuer must never have defaulted on any bond or long-term lease obligation.
D. If the security to be issued is an equity interest in the firm, its offer price has to be at least $5 a

QUESTION 50

Assuming there is not a stop order or a proceeding pending, under the registration by coordination process a security's registration with the state becomes effective:

A. only when it is approved by the state Administrator, regardless of whether it has been approved by the SEC.
B. immediately after approval by the SEC as long as the registration statement has been on file for at least 20 days or the Uniform Securities Act has provided an exemption to this waiting period.
C. immediately subsequent to approval by the SEC, regardless of how long the registration statement has been on file.
D. only when it is approved by the state Administrator, who will review the registration documentation upon notification that SEC approval has been granted.

QUESTION 51

Which of the following is not a method that can be used to register securities with the state?

A. registration by exception
B. registration by notification
C. registration by coordination
D. registration by qualification

QUESTION 52

Which of the following statements regarding "registration by qualification" is true?

A. Registration by qualification refers to the fact that certain categories of securities are exempt from state registration requirements.
B. Registration by qualification is the preferred method used by issuers since it requires the least amount of paperwork.
C. In its simplest form, registration by qualification requires the issuer to supply voluminous amounts of information about both the firm and its directors, officers, and major shareholders.
D. Registration by qualification refers to the fact that the highest quality bonds, i.e., those with a AAA rating, are exempt from registration with the state.

QUESTION 53

Kevin has a pair of season tickets to the Boston Red Sox games. He and his wife can't attend all the games themselves, so Kevin has created "packages" of eight games each that he is listing for sale on Craig's List.

Do these "packages" meet the definition of securities, and, if so, does Kevin need to register them with the state before offering them for sale?

A. If Kevin will be profiting from the sale of the packages, the packages are defined to be securities, but since he's selling the packages to only a few people, he will not have to register them with the state. (Kevin may, however, be guilty of violating ticket scalping laws.)
B. Only if Kevin will be selling the packages at or below cost are the packages not considered to be securities, in which case Kevin will not have to register them with the state.
C. The packages are not considered to be securities since each package is merely a purchase and sale agreement between Kevin and another person. There is no third party involved. Because they do not meet the definition of securities, Kevin does not need to register them with the state.
D. Statements A and B are both true statements.

QUESTION 54

Which of the following securities would be exempt from state registration requirements, according to the Uniform Securities Act?

I. a municipal bond issued by the Canadian province of Nova Scotia
II. a bond issued by the county of Cork, Ireland
III. a bond issued by Nationwide Insurance Company

A. All of the selections would be exempt from state registration requirements under the Uniform
B. Selection I only
C. Selection I and III only
D. Selection III only

QUESTION 55

Which of the following would be considered an "issuer" transaction?

A. Jacob calls his broker and places an order to purchase 100 shares of Hasbro, Inc. on the open market.
B. Maria purchases 500 shares of Dodge and Cox's International Fund, a mutual fund investing in foreign securities.
C. Kim sells an AT&T bond she holds that still has three years remaining to maturity.
D. None of the above is an "issuer" transaction.

QUESTION 56

While on vacation in Colorado, Mr. Moneybags became interested in the stock of a company called SafeAway, which designs and installs customized high-tech security systems in the multimillion dollar mansions located in Colorado's pricier ski resort areas, such as Vail and Aspen. Upon returning to his home in Boston, he calls his broker-dealer with an order to purchase 10,000 shares of the stock, which he learned trades in the over-the-counter market. Fast Eddie, a registered agent with his broker-dealer, discovers that SafeAway's stock is registered only in the states of Colorado and Wyoming. Neither Fast Eddie nor his broker-dealer are registered to do business in either of those states. Under these circumstances,

A. Fast Eddie cannot effect Mr. Moneybags purchase of SafeAway stock since neither he nor his broker are registered to do business in Colorado or Wyoming, and SafeAway stock is not registered for sale in the state of Massachusetts.
B. Fast Eddie can execute the trade for Mr. Moneybags since this would be considered an exempt transaction because it is a private placement.
C. Fast Eddie should contact a broker-dealer that is registered in either Colorado or Wyoming and negotiate a finder's fee for referring Mr. Moneybags to them.
D. Fast Eddie can execute the trade for Mr. Moneybags since this would be considered an exempt transaction because it is an unsolicited transaction.

QUESTION 57

Nancy's Aunt Ethel died, making Nancy executrix of her estate. In going through Aunt Ethel's belongings, Nancy discovered some stock certificates that she learned had been issued by a small New Jersey firm that was still in business. The problem lay in the fact that Nancy's Aunt Ethel had moved from New Jersey to Florida years ago, and the stock is registered only in the state of New Jersey. Nancy herself is a resident of Massachusetts.

What does Nancy have to do in order to sell this stock?

A. Nancy can sell the stock without a problem as executrix of her aunt's estate.
B. Nancy will need to contact a securities law firm in Florida to help her register the stock in the state of Florida.
C. Nancy will need to contact a broker-dealer licensed in the state of New Jersey to help her with the sale of this stock.
D. Nancy will have to establish a mailing address in New Jersey before she can legally sell this stock.

QUESTION 58

Which of the following describes an "exempt security," as defined by the Uniform Securities Act (USA)?

A. An exempt security is any security that is being sold by an institutional investor, such as a bank, to another institutional investor, such as another bank or an insurance company.
B. An exempt security is one that need not be registered in the state in which it is sold.
C. An exempt security is any security being sold as a private placement.
D. An exempt security is any security that is being sold in an isolated non-issuer transaction.

QUESTION 59

Which of the following persons falls under the definition of "broker-dealer," as defined by the Uniform Securities Act (USA)?

A. Marge is a loan officer at Treadwater Bank and Trust.
B. Juan is employed by TrustUs Corporation to sell shares of the firm's stock to the firm's employees and receives a commission on the shares he sells.
C. Michaela is employed by GetErDone broker-dealers and sells both exempt and non-exempt securities to GetErDone's clients.
D. MyTrades is a sole proprietorship owned by Nathan Newmoney, who has established the firm solely to make trades on his own account, thereby avoiding the commissions he would have to pay a middleman.

QUESTION 60

Which of the following persons would not be required to register with the state as an agent under the guidelines of the Uniform Securities Act (USA)?

A. Keith is a salaried employee of Middlesex County in Massachusetts who sells revenue bonds issued by the county to the public.
B. John is employed by TrustUs Corporation to sell shares of the firm's stock to the firm's employees and receives a commission on the shares he sells.
C. Stefan is a sales representative for SecureMoney Broker-Dealers and sells only mutual fund shares.
D. Preetham is part-owner of SecureMoney Broker-Dealers and executes the purchase and sale of securities for the firm's customers.

QUESTION 61

Treadwater Bank and Trust is selling a portfolio of municipal bonds it owns to the SafeRisk Insurance Corporation. Under the Uniform Securities Act (USA), in this transaction Treadwater is defined as a

A. broker-dealer.
B. agent.
C. issuer.
D. none of the above.

QUESTION 62

Under the Uniform Securities Act (USA), the term "investment adviser" does not apply to

I. an investment advisory firm owned and operated by a sole proprietor.
II. a bank or savings institution.
III. an investment adviser representative.
IV. a broker-dealer or its agents if the advice is incidental to the business although there is a nominal charge for any specific investment advice given.

A. I, II, III, or IV.
B. I, II, and III only.
C. II and III only.
D. II, III and IV only.

QUESTION 63

Which of the following statements regarding the registration of broker-dealers and investment advisers is true?

A. Investment advisers are required to register with both the state and the SEC, while broker-dealers may be registered with only one or the other.
B. Investment advisers must always be registered with the SEC to conduct business; broker-dealers may be registered with either an individual state or the SEC or both.
C. Investment advisers are required either to be registered with a state or with the SEC, while broker-dealers must be registered both with the SEC and the state.
D. Both investment advisers and broker-dealers must be registered with the SEC and with the states in which they have offices.

QUESTION 64

Under the Uniform Securities Act (USA), which of the following statements would be disallowed?

A. The government of the U.S. guarantees a 3% interest rate, to be paid semiannually, on a new 5-year Treasury note.
B. A sales representative of GetErDone Broker-Dealers guarantees that a client can expect an average annual rate of return of 2% on a mutual fund investment the sales representative is selling, pointing to the fact that the fund has returned an average annual rate of return of 6% over the past ten years.
C. An insurance company guarantees a fixed payment of $300 a month for life on an annuity it is selling.
D. Neither the statements in Selections B or C would be allowed under the guidelines of the Uniform Securities Act.

QUESTION 65

Which of the following would meet the requirements for an "exempt security?"

A. a $500,000 promissory note that matures in two years
B. commercial paper with a $100,000 face value and a maturity of five months that is rated AA by Standard and Poors
C. a $25,000 promissory note that matures in three months
D. commercial paper with a $200,000 face value and a maturity of three months that is rated BB by Standard and Poors

QUESTION 66

Which of the following describes an investment adviser that is not required to register with the state Administrator?

A. MoeMoney Investment Advisers, LLC has an office in the state with a client base of fifty individuals.
B. Financial Freedom Investment Advisers has no offices in the state although it does advise six wealthy individuals who are residents of the state.
C. CanDo Broker-Dealers is a state-registered broker-dealer. It has begun to offer asset management services to a few of its wealthier clients for a small management fee equal to 0.1% of the assets under management.
D. Buckeye Investment Advisers has no offices in the state, but it provides portfolio management services to an insurance company located in the state.

QUESTION 67

The state official who has regulatory authority over the securities industry within the state is known as the

A. attorney-general.
B. administrator.
C. investor-protection officer.
D. secretary of state.

QUESTION 68

Which of the following actions is the Administrator of a state empowered to take?

A. gather evidence
B. require restitution for the victims of a scam
C. impose civil penalties in cases of fraud
D. The Administrator of a state has the authority to take all of the above actions.

QUESTION 69

Which of the following orders can an Administrator issue without providing prior notice?

A. license suspension
B. license revocation
C. cease and desist
D. license denial

QUESTION 70

It has come to the attention of the Administrator of the state that Samuel Shyster provided false information on his application to become a registered investment adviser with the state. Prior to revoking Samuel's license, the Administrator will provide Samuel with which of the following?

I. prior notice
II. an opportunity to fill out a new registration statement
III. an opportunity for a hearing
IV. a written statement regarding the facts and the legal consequences

A. I, II, III, and IV
B. I, II, and III
C. I, III, and IV
D. I, II, and IV

QUESTION 71

Sam Shyster had his day in court-and lost. His license to do business as an investment adviser in the state has been revoked. What legitimate options does Sam have available to him now?

A. Sam can move to another state and apply for registration as an investment adviser there.
B. Sam has 45 days in which to file an appeal with the attorney general.
C. Sam can register with the SEC as an investment adviser, which will exempt him from state registration requirements.
D. Sam has 60 days to file an appeal of the decision in a court of law.

QUESTION 72

Which of the following constitutes a non-punitive order?

A. summary license suspension
B. registration cancellation
C. registration denial
D. All of the above are punitive orders.

QUESTION 73

Broker-dealer Nebulous opted to withdraw its registration with the state. Six months later, the Administrator finds that Nebulous had been engaged in fraudulent securities transactions.

Which of the following statements is true?

A. The Administrator is unable to take disciplinary action against Nebulous because the self-initiated withdrawal became effective 30 days after the application was filed.
B. The Administrator is only able to take disciplinary action if the misdeeds are discovered within three months of the effective date of the withdrawal, so Nebulous slipped by this time.
C. The Administrator has five years from the discovery of the misdeed to take disciplinary action, so Nebulous will have to be on the lookout for a long time to come.
D. The Administrator can take disciplinary action against Nebulous for up to one year, so Nebulous is in trouble.

QUESTION 74

Broker-Dealer Wheeler has no offices in the state. Wheeler does, however, sell corporate bonds from his portfolio to banks and insurance companies located in the state that purchase the bonds for their investment portfolios. He executes about twelve of these transactions a year. Wheeler profits from the price appreciation of the bonds during the time he held them, but receives no other form of compensation. Based on these facts,

A. Wheeler must register as a broker-dealer in the state, but the securities do not need to be registered.
B. Wheeler need not register in the state, and the securities are also exempt from registration.
C. Wheeler must register as a broker-dealer in the state, and the securities must also be registered before they can be sold to in-state investors.
D. Wheeler need not register in the state, but the securities must be registered before they can be sold to in-state investors.

QUESTION 75

Jack Bean is employed by Giant Investment Advisers, LLC. His job duties include advising clients on the asset allocations of their portfolios. Jack Bean is

A. an investment adviser representative.
B. an investment adviser.
C. an administrative assistant.
D. an agent.

QUESTION 76

Ms. Muffet is employed by Spyder Broker-Dealers. Her job duties include providing price quotes and executing purchases and sales for the firm's clients. She is paid a salary plus commission. Ms. Muffet is

A. a broker-dealer.
B. an agent.
C. an investment adviser.
D. an investment adviser representative.

QUESTION 77

What criminal penalties are specified for "willful violations" of the Uniform Securities Act?

A. license cancellation.
B. license suspension.
C. up to 3 years in prison or a $5,000 fine, or both.
D. up to 5 years in prison or a $10,000 fine, or both.

QUESTION 78

George Geek is a computer programmer who tired of working for others and started his own company. He convinced forty investors that he could design software that would rival Microsoft, and sold them each a 10% partnership interest in his firm for $25,000. He designed and printed up the partnership certificates himself. George told the investors that he had a product that was on the verge of being marketable and that when it did-within the next two months-revenues would pour into the company, and he would begin paying dividends. He told them they could expect a 20% return on their money this year, with even higher returns in the years to come. As it turned out, George wasn't quite the programmer he thought he was, and he wasn't able to get all the bugs out of the program to make it marketable within the promised two months.

Within a year, George had tired of the project and was too busy picking up chicks in his new Corvette when he wasn't on the island of St. Bart overseeing the construction of his new beach mansion-and picking up chicks. His activities, of course, were financed by the extremely generous "salary" he paid himself from the investors' monies.

Under the Uniform Securities Act, do the investors have any civil claims against George?

A. Yes. They can sue George for the return of their original investment, plus interest. George would also have to pay their court costs and attorneys' fees and any amounts assessed by the court for "pain and suffering" on the parts of the clients.
B. No. It wasn't George's fault that he was unable to do what he promised. Even if it wasn't for.
C. Yes. They can sue George for the return of their original investment, plus interest. George would.
D. No. The Uniform Securities Act only involves securities laws and partnership interests are not.

QUESTION 79

Ms. Naiveté gave Mr. Smooth, owner of Smooth Construction, $40,000 in return for a promissory note that promised to pay interest at the rate of 8% a quarter, with a repayment of principal at the end of two years. The money would be used by Mr. Smooth to rehab a few beach condo units that had been severely hurricane- damaged and that Mr. Smooth had been able to purchase for "pennies on the dollar," or so he said. The first units would be completed within a month, and the rents would be used to make the interest payments. The investment was almost as risk-free as U.S. government bonds, Mr. Smooth claimed. By the end of the second year, Ms. Naiveté had received a lot of fast talk and only one of the promised interest payments.

Have there been any violation of securities laws in this instance?

A. No. This was simply a loan transacted between two parties.
B. Yes. Mr. Smooth was required to register the promissory note before he offered it for sale.
C. Yes. Ms. Naiveté has been defrauded by Mr. Smooth.
D. Both B and C are true statements.

QUESTION 80

You have recently discovered that a security you purchased has not been registered with the state, nor is it exempt from registration. You can file a civil claim against the seller as long as you do so within

A. five years.
B. three years from discovery or five years from the event, whichever comes first.
C. two years from discovery or three years from the event, whichever comes first.
D. one year from discovery.

QUESTION 81

Iggy recently started his own company. He soon discovered it required more cash to keep it going than he had anticipated. He ran an ad in the local paper for investors and got a response. He found a template for a promissory note on the internet, filled in the requisite information specific to the agreement he and the investor had worked out, and printed it out. On it, he promised to make monthly interest payments of 2% on the loan and to repay the principal amount at the end of 18 months. A few months after the arrangement, Iggy read an article in a small business publication that indicated that promissory notes had to be registered with the state unless they were sold in an exempt transaction, such as one enacted with a financial institution, prior to being offered for sale. The article indicated that a seller who had sold an unregistered note in error could remedy the situation by sending the buyer a formal offer to buy the security back, with interest. Iggy turned to the computer once again, found a form that could be used for a formal offer of rescission, filled it out, and sent it to the investor. Having done this,

A. Iggy cannot be sued for civil damages if the investor fails to respond to the offer within 30 days.
B. Iggy must follow up with a second notice sent via registered mail if he has not heard from the investor within 30 days.
C. Iggy must wait 6 months for a response from the investor. If no response is received by the end of 6 months, Iggy is off the hook.
D. Iggy will not be assessed any penalties by the Administrator of the state, but the investor can still sue for damages in civil court.

QUESTION 82

An investment adviser suggests that his client, Arnold, a 74-year old gentleman, should consider a reallocation of the assets in his portfolio. The adviser tells Arnold that he has far too much invested in bonds, which don't earn as much as stocks. He advises Arnold to take 80% of the money he has in bonds and invest it in an aggressive growth mutual fund that has provided an average annual return of 40% over the past three years. Arnold is impressed and follows this advice. Shortly thereafter, there is a steep drop in the market in general, and the net asset value of the aggressive growth mutual fund falls 85%.

Does Arnold have any remedies available to him?

A. No. Arnold had the choice and got greedy. As the old saying goes, "Bulls get rich, and bears get rich, but pigs get led to slaughter."
B. Yes. Arnold can sue for the amount of his losses, plus interest, as well as an amount assessed by the court for "pain and suffering."
C. No. The investment adviser had no way of knowing that the market was going to fall when he provided the advice, so the adviser did not fail in his fiduciary responsibility to Arnold.
D. Yes. Arnold can sue for the amount of his losses, plus interest, court costs, and attorneys' fees.

QUESTION 83

Julia Hasty has recently applied with the Administrator to be a registered investment adviser in the state. Eager to open her new business, she has business cards printed that indicate that she is a "state-registered" investment adviser and visits some local businesses, asking them for permission to put some of her cards in their waiting rooms.

Has Julia violated any of the provisions of the Uniform Securities Act by distributing her business cards?

A. No. As long as her application has been submitted and is pending acceptance, Julia has not violated any provisions of the Uniform Securities Act.
B. No. The provisions of the Uniform Securities Act relate to securities, not people.
C. Yes. Julia is not permitted to advertise as a "state-registered" investment adviser until she receives notification of the acceptance of her application by the state Administrator.
D. No. Julia has merely put her business cards in waiting rooms. She has not opened her business to clients yet.

QUESTION 84

Ari Gaunt is employed by a small state-registered broker-dealer and has recently received notification that his application to be a registered agent of the state has been accepted. Now that he is licensed to execute transactions for the firm's clients, Ari has a batch of business cards printed up, with a picture of himself on the right-hand side of the card. Underneath the picture is the caption, "State-Approved Agent." Will Ari be violating any securities laws if he distributes these business cards?

A. No. However, he may be violating company policy of the broker-dealer he works for by designing his own cards.
B. No. His registration with the Administrator of the state has been accepted, so he is entitled to call himself a "State-Approved Agent."
C. Yes. Agents are not permitted to include a picture of themselves on their business cards.
D. Yes. It is a violation of a securities law to suggest that he has been approved by the state Administrator.

QUESTION 85

Which of the following is not in itself a reason for the Administrator to deny, suspend, or revoke the license of a person?

A. The applicant has never before worked in the securities industry although he has received the requisite training.
B. Some of the information supplied on the registration application was found to be false.
C. The person has been convicted of check kiting within the past ten years.
D. The person is a broker-dealer whose agents have repeatedly been accused of churning and burning, according to written client complaints.

QUESTION 86

Once a person has filed an application with the Administrator, and in doing so has truthfully disclosed every material fact, how long does the Administrator have after the effective date of the registration to commence a proceeding to deny, suspend, or revoke that person's license based on those facts?

A. 30 days.
B. 60 days.
C. 90 days.
D. one year.

QUESTION 87

A broker-dealer cannot legally be

A. a partnership.
B. an individual.
C. a sole-proprietorship.
D. A broker-dealer can be any of the above.

QUESTION 88

Harry Lange manages the investment portfolio for the Fidelity Magellan Mutual Fund. Mr. Lange is a(n)

A. broker-dealer.
B. agent.
C. investment adviser.
D. investment company.

QUESTION 89

An investment adviser

I. provides investment advice to clients.
II. sells securities to clients.
III. buys and sells securities in their clients' accounts for the clients.

A. I only.
B. I and II only.
C. I and III only.
D. I, II, and III.

QUESTION 90

After passing the necessary exams, you must submit which of the following to the state Administrator when applying for registration as an agent?

A. U-4
B. Form ADV
C. a recent photograph of yourself
D. proof that you meet the state's minimum net capital requirement

QUESTION 91

Bootstraps, Inc. is a family-owned business that has experienced enormous growth in the last couple of years. The business needs more cash to support this growth and has decided to issue some promissory notes, each with a face value of $5,000, for sale to the general public. The firm plans to hire three individuals to help them sell these notes. These individuals will earn a commission based on the notes they sell.

Given these facts, which of the following is true?

A. The notes must be registered with the state, and the three individuals hired to sell the notes must be registered as agents with the state.
B. The notes must be registered with the state, but the individuals hired to sell them are not required to be registered.
C. Neither the notes nor the individuals selling the notes need to be registered with the state.
D. Either the firm must register the notes with the state, or the individuals that are hired to sell the notes must be registered as agents with the state, but not both.

QUESTION 92

Skip is a registered agent with state. He recently quit his job with Venus Broker-Dealers to become affiliated with

Mars Broker-Dealers. Which of the three entities must report this change to the state Administrator?

A. Skip only
B. Skip and either Mars or Venus, but not both
C. Both Skip and Venus
D. Skip, Mars, and Venus

QUESTION 93

The net worth of a broker-dealer has fallen below the minimum net capital requirement specified by the state in which the broker-dealer is registered. This broker- dealer must notify the Administrator of this fact

A. before the beginning of the next quarter.
B. before the end of the month.
C. by the close of business on the next business day.
D. within a week's time.

QUESTION 94

Barring no irregularities (such as a license revocation by another state last year), after you have filed for registration as an agent, your license will be granted within

A. 10 business days.
B. 14 business days.
C. 30 days.
D. 45 days.

QUESTION 95

S. White and Associates is an investment adviser registered in the state of Kentucky and, as such, is meeting Kentucky's minimum net capital requirement for investment advisers. The firm recently registered with the state of Virginia and has opened an office there. Virginia has a significantly higher net capital requirement for its investment advisers.

Which of the following statements is true?

A. According to the Uniform Securities Act, S. White will have to meet Virginia's higher requirement.
B. According to the Investment Advisers Act of 1940, S. White needs only to meet the net capital requirement of Kentucky.
C. According to the Securities Exchange Act of 1934, S. White needs to meet at least the minimum net capital requirement specified by that Act since it is now operating in multiple states.
D. According to the Investment Advisers Act of 1940, S. White will have to maintain a minimum net capital equal to the average of the net capital requirements of the two states.

QUESTION 96

Which of the following statements is false?

A. A state cannot require a higher minimum net capital for broker-dealers than the amount specified by the Securities Exchange Act of 1934.
B. A state cannot require a higher minimum net capital for investment advisers than the amount specified by the Investment Advisers Act of 1940.
C. The minimum net capital requirement for investment advisers that take custody of their clients' assets is higher than the net capital requirement for advisers who do not take custody of the assets.
D. None of the above statements is false; all are true statements.

QUESTION 97

Which of the following entities are subject to post-registration provisions?

I. broker-dealers
II. agents
III. investment advisers
IV. investment adviser representatives

A. I and II only
B. I and III only
C. II and IV only
D. All of the entities are subject to post-registration provisions.

QUESTION 98

Fly-By-Night Investment Advisers has closed its doors. Which of the following statements is true?

A. Fly-By-Night is required to shred all documentation of client transactions and communications.
B. Fly-By-Night must send all records of client transactions and communications to the state Administrator for safekeeping.
C. Fly-By-Night must preserve and maintain all records, including client transactions and communications, advertising materials, and financial statements of the now-defunct business for five years.
D. Fly-By-Night must send each of its former clients its records of all that client's transactions and communications with the firm over the past five years.

QUESTION 99

You have passed the necessary exams (congratulations!) and are applying for registration as a securities agent. It is already the end of September. Therefore, you must pay

A. one-fourth of the annual fee required since only one quarter of the year remains.
B. the full annual fee, and your license will expire on September 30th next year.
C. the full annual fee, and your license will expire on December 31st next year.
D. the full annual fee, and your license will expire on December 31st this year.

QUESTION 100

To continue operating as an agent, broker-dealer, investment adviser, or investment adviser representative next year, you must pay the filing fee to renew your license with the state Administrator by

A. January 15th of the new year.
B. January 30th of the new year.
C. December 31st of this year.
D. the anniversary date of the original issue date on your license.

QUESTION 101

Mr. Bigwig, CEO of HiGrowth Corporation, meets with the president of BigFee Investment Bankers and arranges for BigFee to underwrite an Initial Public Offering (IPO) for the firm. When the IPO comes to market, GetErDone Broker-Dealers is part of the selling group, which handles the sale of the stock to the public.

In this scenario, which party is acting as a dealer?

A. HiGrowth Corporation
B. Mr. Bigwig
C. BigFee Investment Bankers
D. GetErDone Broker-Dealers

QUESTION 102

Mr. Bigwig, CEO of HiGrowth Corporation, meets with the president of BigFee Investment Bankers and arranges for BigFee to underwrite an Initial Public Offering (IPO) for the firm. When the IPO comes to market, GetErDone Broker-Dealers is part of the selling group, which handles the sale of the stock to the public.

In this scenario, which party is the broker?

A. HiGrowth Corporation
B. Mr. Bigwig
C. BigFee Investment Bankers
D. GetErDone Broker-Dealers

QUESTION 103

A bond issue has recently been registered with the state Administrator. Which of the following statements are true?

A. An investor can feel secure in buying the bond because it has recently been registered, which means that the state Administrator finds it to be of sound quality at this point in time.
B. The bond may now be offered for sale in the state.
C. The issuer may now offer this bond for sale, and any other bonds that the issuer may want to offer for sale in the future will be able be sold after the issuer executes a notice filing.
D. Both A and B are true statements.

QUESTION 104

BondsRUs is a broker-dealer that (unsurprisingly) specializes in bonds. The firm has found that it is able to sell Treasury bonds that it buys for $90 per $100 of par value for $99 per $100 of par value to some of its more naïve clients, who never pay attention to the confirmation statements BondsRUs sends them. BondsRUs is guilty of

A. nothing. It is acting as a dealer in bonds and, as such, can charge its clients whatever the clients are willing to pay.
B. overcharging its clients by unreasonable markups. A $9 dealer's spread on Treasury bonds is unwarranted.
C. fraud.
D. both B and C.

QUESTION 105

A broker-dealer of commodity futures contracts has been profiting by trading for its own account either before or after executing a client's trade on the same commodity, depending on which will be most advantageous. Under the Uniform Securities Act, the broker-dealer is guilty of

A. fraud.
B. churning.
C. unauthorized transactions.
D. nothing. The Uniform Securities Act (USA) deals only with securities, and a commodity futures contract is not a security.

QUESTION 106

The Turnover Corporation, a firm with 25,000 employees, has recently hired 50 new employees, many of whom have been hired to replace middle-level managers who have retired. Turnover has omitted this fact from its prospectus. Turnover is guilty of

A. fraud.
B. misrepresentation.
C. misusing insider information.
D. nothing. The hiring of 50 new employees by a firm with 25,000 employees is not a material fact.

QUESTION 107

In its prospectus, the YourMoney Mutual Fund provides charts and tables of its average annual return over the past year, three years, five years, and ten years. The fund's return has indeed been phenomenal over this time period, beating the S&P 500 Index by at least 15%. The prospectus states that this is because the fund invests in securities that are riskier and that, therefore, an investor can expect the fund to continue earning a return higher than the S&P 500 Index.

Is YourMoney guilty of any security violations?

A. No. YourMoney properly revealed to prospective investors the fact that its higher than average returns are the result of its investment in riskier securities.
B. Yes. There is no way the fund could have beaten the S&P 500 Index by at least 15% over the past ten years. The fund is obviously misstating its returns.
C. Yes. YourMoney is guilty of fraud in claiming that "an investor can expect the fund to continue earning a return higher than the S&P 500 Index." Past performance is no indication of future performance.
D. No. Regulations require only that the mutual fund provide charts and tables of its average annual returns, with a statement comparing the fund performance with a relevant market index. YourMoney has done this and more.

QUESTION 108

Constance is an investment adviser representative. She told one of her clients that he should put at least 15% of his investment monies in a U.S. government bond mutual fund.
She explained that she believed that he required this percentage to meet his liquidity needs, and U.S. government bond funds are risk-free. A few months later, the client needed to sell some of his fund shares in order to pay some medical bills and was surprised to discover that he lost money on the sale because the net asset value of the fund had dropped.

Was Constance guilty of any securities violations?

A. Yes. Constance is guilty of fraud. She misled the client into thinking he couldn't lose any money if he invested the money in a U.S. government bond mutual fund.
B. Yes. Constance should never recommend that a client invest such a high percentage of his investment monies in a U.S. government bond mutual fund.
C. No. U.S. government bonds are often referred to as risk-free investments, so Constance made no misstatement of fact in telling her client this.
D. It depends. If Constance realized that the client could lose money in a U.S. government bond fund, then she is guilty of fraud, but if she did not herself realize that, then she is merely misinformed.

QUESTION 109

D. Vious and Associates is a small broker-dealer trying to generate more business. To this end, the firm had a professional four-color brochure printed that provides the years of industry experience of its management along with other information. The firm's founder, Ms. D. Vious, is listed as having over 30 years of experience in the industry. Ms. D. Vious has worked for broker-dealers for over 30 years, but for 20 of those 30 years, she was a secretary.

Has D. Vious violated any securities laws?

A. No. Technically, Ms. D. Vious does have over 30 years of experience in the industry, even though it was not in the capacity of an agent or a broker-dealer.
B. No. Ms. D. Vious' years of experience is not a material fact that would affect an investor's investment decision.
C. Yes. The broker-dealer is making a misleading statement in an advertising brochure in order to convince investors to do business with the firm.
D. No. Advertising brochures are not securities.

QUESTION 110

In which of the following cases is an investment adviser allowed to be compensated with a share of the capital gains of the client's portfolio?

I. The client is a mutual fund.
II. The client is a credit union.
III. The client is a private client whose minimum net worth is $1 million or more.
IV. The client is a private client who has at least $750,000 invested through the investment adviser.

A. I and II only
B. I, II, and III only
C. I, II, and IV only
D. none of the above. An investment adviser is never allowed to share in the capital gains earned on

QUESTION 111

Alter Advisers & Associates is a small investment adviser partnership registered only in a single state. One of the partners has died, and the surviving spouse has sold that partnership interest to the surviving partners.

Which of the following statements are true?

I. Alter Advisers must inform the state Administrator of this event.
II. Alter Advisers must inform the SEC of this event.
III. Alter Advisers must notify the firm's clients of this event.

A. I only
B. I and II only
C. I and III only
D. I, II, and III

QUESTION 112

Switch Advisory is a small investment adviser partnership registered in a single state. A larger investment adviser firm, Bait Investment Adviser, is registered in the same state as well as two other states. Bait has offered to buy out three of Switch's partners who want to retire. This will give Bait a 60% ownership in Switch Advisory.

Which of the following statements are true?

I. Switch Advisory must obtain the approval of its clients before the partners can sell their interests to Bait.
II. Switch Advisory must notify the state Administrator of this event.
III. Switch Advisory must notify their clients of this event, but does not need the clients' approval.
IV. Switch Advisory must notify the SEC of this event.

A. I only
B. I and II only
C. II, III, and IV only
D. I, II, and IV only

QUESTION 113

Noah Aull is an investment adviser representative with Canto Investment Advisers. A client has called and told Noah that he heard about a firm that had recently completed an IPO at a party he had attended that weekend and instructed Noah to purchase shares of the company, which was now trading on the OTC Bulletin Board. Noah did some research and felt the company was far too risky an investment for this client, so he did not execute the trade. This turned out to be fortunate for his client since the firm became insolvent within six months of its IPO.

Has Noah done anything wrong?

A. Yes. Noah is guilty of misappropriation and could have his license revoked.
B. No. Noah did what he is hired to do-manage his clients' accounts to the best of his ability.
C. Yes. Noah is guilty of not following a client's instructions and could have his license revoked.
D. Yes. Noah is guilty of making an unauthorized transaction and could have his license revoked.

QUESTION 114

Mr. and Mrs. Cleaver are nearing retirement and have made an appointment with Mr. Eddie, an investment adviser representative who works for Haskell Investment Advisers, to get advice on how they can better structure their investments to meet their retirement goals. Their son, Theodore, who has recently graduated college and has a great job as a software writer for a video game company, accompanies them. Mr. Eddie explains that the main goal of any plan is diversification and recommends that Mr. and Mrs. Cleaver spread their investment monies equally among six load mutual funds that Mr. Eddie can sell them. He suggests that Theodore follow suit and invest any monies he has equally among the same ten funds.

Has Mr. Eddie done anything wrong?

A. Yes. Mr. Eddie has advised his clients to invest in load funds when no load funds are clearly better investments.
B. No. Diversification should, in fact, be the goal, and he has advised a well-diversified plan for his clients.
C. Yes. Clients who are ready to retire have different investment needs than a client who is just entering the work force. The recommendation that both Theodore and his parents have the same asset allocation is clearly unsuitable.
D. Yes. Mr. Eddie is guilty of misappropriation, a prohibited practice.

QUESTION 115

Stu Pede is an agent with broker-dealer Cavalier. A customer calls with a request to establish a classic IRA and asks for Stu's advice regarding where the money in the IRA should be invested. Stu suggests a municipal bond fund, explaining to his client that the interest income earned on it will be tax-free at the federal level, and some of it may even be tax-free at the state and local levels.

Has Stu engaged in any prohibited practices?

A. Yes. Stu is an agent with a broker-dealer. He is not an investment adviser representative and is not allowed to make recommendations regarding investments to the firm's clients.
B. No. Although Stu has given investment advice, it was solicited by the client, and Stu received no additional compensation for the advice.
C. Yes. Municipal bonds are not suitable investments for a classic IRA, and Stu can have his license revoked or suspended.
D. No. Although municipal bonds are not suitable investments for a classic IRA, Stu obviously didn't know this and is merely guilty of stupidity.

QUESTION 116

Ken Con is an agent with Blue Sky Broker-Dealers. He gets up early each morning so that he can study any late-breaking news that may affect the markets and figure out ways to incorporate this news into conversations with select clients in order to pressure them to restructure their portfolios by selling holdings they have in one particular industry to invest the money in another particular industry.

Ken has been very successful with this strategy and executes more trades for his clients than any other agent with the firm, but is he in danger of losing his license?

A. Yes. Ken is engaging in churning, a prohibited practice and can have his license revoked or suspended.
B. It depends. If his clients have lost money, Ken may lose his license; but if a review indicates that his clients' accounts earn profits, then his license is safe.
C. Yes. Ken is guilty of the prohibited practice of "tailgating."
D. No. Ken is just a successful sales person who is working harder than the other agents in the firm.

QUESTION 117

Mr. Sailor is cruising through the Bahamas when he learns that a healthcare company in which he owns stock is being sued by former patients, doctors, nurses, and even the federal government. He doesn't have his broker's number handy, and he doesn't have internet access, so he calls his son and tells him to call the broker and instruct the broker to sell his shares. As a registered agent for his broker, you take the call.

Should you execute this transaction?

A. Yes. This is a legitimate request from a client, and you are required to follow the client's instructions.
B. No, not unless you and your broker-dealer have a written document that gives Mr. Sailor's son the power-of-attorney to trade on his account.
C. Yes, as long as the son presents proper identification that proves his relationship to Mr. Sailor, such as a birth certificate.
D. Yes, as long as the son is at least 21 years old and not a minor child.

QUESTION 118

You are an investment adviser to Mr. Crochety, an elderly man who lives solely on his social security income although he managed to accumulate an investment portfolio worth about $100,000 over the years. Mr. Crochety recently got his hands on a business publication and read about the tax-free interest paid by municipal bonds. He calls you and instructs you to sell his other investments and invest all his money in a municipal bond portfolio, so that "the government doesn't get any more of my hard-earned money." You tell Mr. Crochety that you don't believe this is a wise move because he's in such a low tax bracket that municipal bonds are not a good investment for him, but he is insistent. Based on these facts, you should

A. ignore Mr. Crochety's instruction since it is not in his best interest.
B. require Mr. Crochety to sign an affidavit of liability waiver, indicating that you will not be held responsible for any adverse consequences of this decision.
C. have Mr. Crochety sign a statement of investment policy that indicates that this transaction is being executed on the client's instructions and that you have advised the client against it.
D. call Mr. Crochety's relatives and suggest they have him examined for mental instability.

QUESTION 119

A broker-dealer will be found guilty of churning an account if the account has a turnover ratio of

A. four.
B. five.
C. eight.
D. There is no specified turnover ratio assigned to the prohibited practice of churning.

QUESTION 120

Goldie Locks is an agent with Bear Broker-Dealers. One of her clients is a single woman, Annie Spinster, who is retired and needs income from her investment portfolio to meet her current needs for liquidity. In addition to investing in mutual funds, Annie likes the thrill of investing in single stocks and asks Goldie for recommendations. Goldie recommends Annie invest some of her money in Alcon (ACL), a medical instrument and supplies company selling on the NYSE, based on the fact that it has a high dividend yield and is paying a dividend of $2.21 a share, which is guaranteed to continue or even increase, Goldie assures Annie.

Has Goldie violated any laws or engaged in any prohibited practices?

A. Yes. At the very least, Goldie has committed fraud since she cannot guarantee that a firm's dividend will continue or increase.
B. Yes. As the agent of a broker-dealer, Goldie is not permitted to make recommendations for specific investments. Only investment adviser representatives and investment advisers can do that.
C. No. Goldie merely responded to a recommendation request from a client, and the recommendation is suitable since the client has a need for current income and the recommended stock pays a high dividend.
D. Both A and B are true.

QUESTION 121

Mr. L. Ranger is an agent for a broker-dealer and has overheard "talk" that a merger between two well-known high-tech companies is about to take place. Mr. Ranger knows that, on average, in these instances the target firm's price spikes. He calls his client and good friend, Mr. Tonto, and tells him of the rumor, suggesting that Tonto might want to buy shares in the target firm. He tells Mr. Tonto that if the rumor isn't true, the target firm's price may not spike at all and may, in fact, decline, and suggests that Mr. Tonto not invest any money he isn't willing to lose. Mr. Ranger knows that his friend likes to gamble, and decided he wouldn't be much of a friend if he didn't inform Tonto of this potential opportunity.

Has Mr. L. Ranger violated any laws or engaged in any prohibited practices?

A. No. Mr. Ranger and Mr. Tonto are friends, so there can be no violations of any laws or practices because of their non-business relationship.
B. Yes. Mr. Ranger has engaged in fraud in telling Mr. Tonto about the rumor, given that the merger hasn't been officially announced by the two companies.
C. No. Mr. Ranger has informed Mr. Tonto that the merger is just a rumor and has informed him of the risk involved. Mr. Ranger is knowledgeable about his friend's risk tolerance level as well and recognizes this investment as one his good friend might want to take.
D. Yes. Mr. Ranger is privy to knowledge that is not available to the general public and both he and Mr. Tonto will be guilty of illegal insider trading if Mr. Tonto trades on Mr. Ranger's information.

QUESTION 122

Joe Treader is the owner of a small, state-registered investment advisory firm that is on the verge of becoming insolvent. One of his clients who has become like a mother to him is aware of his financial difficulties and has offered to sell off some of the assets that he manages for her and loan him the money to get him through this period of economic uncertainty until he is able to get on his feet again.

Can Joe take her up on her offer?

A. Yes. Based on the facts presented, it is an unsolicited offer and, as such, Joe can (and should) accept it.
B. Yes, but only if Joe draws up a formal loan agreement with a fair interest rate, based on the going market rates, stated in the agreement as well as a firm date for principal repayment.
C. No. As the client's investment adviser, he has a fiduciary relationship with the client. Entering a loan agreement with this client could lead to conflicts of interest.
D. Both A and B are true.

QUESTION 123

The state of Massachusetts has issued a general obligation (G.O.) bond that pays 3% interest. As an agent selling this bond, you can legitimately tell the investor that

A. the bond is guaranteed by the state of Massachusetts and is, therefore, a risk-free investment.
B. the interest income the investor receives from the bond will be free from federal taxation.
C. all state general obligation bonds are also guaranteed by the federal government.
D. all of the above statements are true.

QUESTION 124

Jack and Jill are a newly married couple in their mid-20s. They are determined to retire by the time they are 50 and have arranged a meeting with a representative of Professional Investment Advisers to structure a financial plan that will allow them to achieve this goal.

The representative, Mr. Hill, advises them to invest at least 60% of their money in bond funds to minimize the risk of loss on the way to their goal. Mr. Hill has

A. made an unsuitable recommendation for these clients and is subject to license suspension or revocation.
B. advised Jack and Jill well with a conservative allocation of their money to preserve principal.
C. committed fraud in indicating that bonds are less risky than stocks.
D. has committed fraud in promoting their delusion that they can possibly expect to retire by the time they turn 50, regardless of their investment strategy.

QUESTION 125

Finn Nance has recently passed his CFP exam and is now a certified financial planner. He has new business cards printed that have the words "Certified Financial Planner" printed under his picture. In doing so,

A. Finn has not violated any laws or engaged in any prohibited practices.
B. Finn has violated a securities law. The Uniform Securities Act prohibits anyone from using the word "certified" on any advertisement for services.
C. Finn has possibly violated a state securities regulation. The Administrator in many states prohibits the use of the word "certified" on any advertisement for services.
D. Finn is not in violation of any laws as long as he has notified the state Administrator of his new designation and his new logo.

QUESTION 126

Elizabeth is the owner of Lizbeth Investment Advisers, a small, state-registered investment advisory firm. She has decided that her firm needs a niche and has learned that a consulting group is coming to the area and offering a 3-day seminar on asset allocation for senior citizens offered by Advantage for Retirement Persons (ARP). The seminar will cost $1,000 per individual, but after attending the seminar, each attendee will receive a certificate verifying their involvement in the program. Elizabeth decides this is the niche she has been looking for and signs up herself and her three investment adviser representatives for the program. After attending the seminar and receiving their certificates, Elizabeth and her team can

A. represent themselves as certified senior citizen investment advisers.
B. have the words "Senior-Citizen Investment Specialists" printed on their business cards.
C. indicate that they are certified by the ARP program since money was paid for their attendance.
D. do none of the above.

QUESTION 127

Penny Swyne, an agent employed by Bear Broker-Dealers, has received a written complaint via e-mail from Mr.

Wolf regarding her performance as his agent. What are Ms. Swyne's legitimate options?

A. Ms. Swyne can call Mr. Wolf and offer to meet him for a romantic dinner and try to convince him to revoke the complaint.
B. As illegal as it may sound, since the complaint was via e-mail, Ms. Swyne can hit the delete button and make it all go away.
C. Ms. Swyne must forward the complaint to the state Administrator.
D. Ms. Swyne must provide Bear Broker-Dealers with a copy of the complaint.

QUESTION 128

You are employed as an agent with CanDo Broker-Dealers. Your brother is software engineer with VideoMagic. When you were talking to him on the phone the other day, he told you that he overheard a conversation by some of the firm's executives that indicated that VideoMagic was about to take over another software company.

Which of the following would violate insider trading rules?

I. The next day, you get an unsolicited call from a client requesting that you sell his shares in Video Magic, and you execute the trade.
II. You buy stock in Video Magic's target firm in anticipation that its stock price will rise when the information becomes public.
III. You recommend the stock of Video Magic's target firm to investors based on the fact that, on average, the stock price of target firms increases.

A. I, II and III
B. I and II only
C. I and III only
D. II and III only

QUESTION 129

Mr. Teche is an agent with broker-dealer CanDo, and his only compensation is the commissions he earns on trades he executes. He has applied for and been granted an adjunct teaching position with a local university that will allow him to earn money while he is establishing himself.

Which of the following statements are true?

A. As an agent with broker-dealer CanDo, Mr. Teche must notify CanDo in writing of this position prior to accepting it.
B. CanDo can deny Mr. Teche permission to accept the adjunct teaching position.
C. Mr. Teche is, in essence, an independent contractor with broker-dealer CanDo and can engage in any other business activity at will.
D. Both A and B are true.

QUESTION 130

Which of the following would be an unsuitable recommendation for your 68-year-old client?

A. a Treasury Inflation Protected Security (TIPS)
B. a deferred annuity
C. an S&P 500 Index mutual fund
D. a high quality corporate bond fund

QUESTION 131

Which of the following is an example of commingling?

A. Sly is an agent with a broker-dealer who recently executed a stock purchase for his client and had the client make the check for the purchase out to Sly for deposit in Sly's broker-dealer account.
B. In order to generate more commissions for herself Ms. Fox makes trades on some of her client's accounts and has the trade confirmations sent to a P.O box she owns.
C. Mr. Hawk encourages his clients to leave their securities in "street name" with the broker-dealer for which Mr. Hawk works.
D. All of the above are examples of commingling.

QUESTION 132

You are an agent with a broker-dealer and have learned of limited partnership interests being sold by a small company that is planning to come out with a product that you think is going to "wow" the market. You would like to get in on the action, but the minimum investment needed is $10,000, and you don't have that kind of dough lying around. You talk to your brother, who is also one of your clients, and get him interested in investing in the firm, too. The two of you decide to pull your money together, each putting in $5,000, and you agree to split any profits or losses.

Is this permitted?

A. No. Under no circumstances can an agent enter a joint investment with a client under the guidelines of the Uniform Securities Act.
B. Yes. This is permitted since the agreement is between you and a family member.
C. Maybe. But it will require written consent from both your brother and your firm.
D. Yes, as long as your brother provides your firm with his written consent.

QUESTION 133

Your next-door neighbor's brother works for a large pharmaceutical company and confided in her that one of the company's chemists has just discovered a compound that will cure baldness and that the firm plans to make the discovery public later in the week. Your next-door neighbor passes this information on to you over a cup of coffee the next morning. You immediately call your broker and place an order to buy shares of the company's stock.

Has any illegal insider trading taken place?

A. Yes. The agent who executes your purchase order has engaged in illegal insider trading.
B. No. You are in no way related to your next-door neighbor's brother, and she could have been lying.
C. Yes. You, your neighbor, and her brother are all guilty of illegal insider trading.
D. Yes. You are guilty of illegal insider trading because you traded on information that had not yet been made publicly available.

QUESTION 134

You are an investment adviser representative. Your client, Mr. I. M. Pulse, calls you with what he thinks is exciting news. He just passed a restaurant and saw Microsoft's Bill Gates having lunch with a local entrepreneur who owns a small firm in the computer software industry that trades on the OTC pink sheets. He is sure that this means Microsoft is negotiating a purchase of the smaller company and instructs you to take the cash balance in his account and buy shares of the local company. You should

A. tell Mr. I.M. Pulse that this would be an illegal insider trade and that you are unable to fulfill his request.
B. call your supervisor and alert him immediately of Mr. Pulse's attempt to have you place an illegal order on his behalf in case Mr. Pulse decides to place the order elsewhere.
C. advise Mr. Pulse that he may be jumping the gun, but place the order if he insists.
D. do both A and B.

QUESTION 135

Mina is a new agent with SecureMoney Broker-Dealers and is struggling to make ends meet. She gets a job as a receptionist at a fitness club on the weekends to generate more income.

Which of the following is true?

A. Mina should have notified SecureMoney in writing before signing on to work at the fitness club.
B. Because the job as a receptionist at a fitness club has nothing to do with the world of finance, Mina has done nothing inappropriate.
C. Mina simply needs to tell her immediate supervisor at SecureMoney about her new job.
D. Mina needs to send notice to the state Administrator informing him of her extracurricular activity.

QUESTION 136

Which of the following would not appear on an order ticket?

A. the stock symbol
B. the account number of the client buying or selling the security
C. the settlement date
D. the agent's commission

QUESTION 137

Rich Quick is a broker-dealer registered in the state of Massachusetts. He occasionally trades on abnormalities he observes in bond yield spreads for his own account, short selling a bond that appears to be overpriced based on its yield and buying a bond that is identical in almost every respect except for the price, which is less than that of the other bond. He has been able to earn arbitrage profits 95% of the time when he does this. Rich Quick

A. is in violation of securities laws. Arbitrage is a prohibited activity.
B. is skilled if he is able to earn profits 95% of the time using this strategy.
C. is trading on insider information, which is a violation of securities laws.
D. engaged in a fraudulent activity.

QUESTION 138

Which of the following would not appear on a trade confirmation?

A. the client's account number
B. the commission
C. the settlement date
D. All of the above items appear on a trade confirmation.

QUESTION 139

The trade confirmation must be received by the customer no later than

A. one week after the settlement date.
B. the settlement date.
C. the day after the trade takes place.
D. five business days after the settlement date.

QUESTION 140

The settlement date refers to

A. the date the order to purchase or sell the security is sent to the market.
B. the date the buyer must pay for the securities purchased.
C. the date the order to purchase or sell a security is actually executed. This may differ from the date that the order is sent to the market in the cases of limit or stop orders.
D. the latest date on which broker-dealers can file their quarterly financial statements with the Administrator of the state.

QUESTION 141

Alice Wonder called her broker on Tuesday, August 10th, with a market order to buy 10 calls on the stock of Abbott Laboratories. Under normal conditions, Alice will have to pay for the calls on

A. Wednesday, August 11th.
B. Tuesday, August 10th.
C. Friday, August 13th.
D. Monday, August 16th.

QUESTION 142

Your client calls you with a market order to purchase 500 shares of the stock of Oracle and asks when payment will be due. If today is Wednesday, September 15th, you inform the client that payment is due on

A. Monday, September 20th.
B. Thursday, September 16th.
C. Friday, September 17th.
D. Saturday, September 18th.

QUESTION 143

You execute a stock transaction for a client on Thursday, September 23rd. The settlement date on the order ticket will be

A. Thursday, September 23rd.
B. Monday, September 27th.
C. Friday, September 24th.
D. Tuesday, September 28th.

QUESTION 144

Today's edition of the Wall Street Journal carried a front page story regarding a federal lawsuit that has been filed against a software manufacturer for monopolistic practices. The CFO of the company called his broker today and sold some of the shares he owns in the company.

Which of the following statements are true?

I. The CFO is guilty of illegal insider trading.
II. If the agent who effected the transaction for the CFO knew he was CFO of the software company, the agent is guilty of illegal insider trading.
III. The broker-dealer for whom the agent works may have its license suspended or revoked if its agent has knowingly executed this illegal insider trade for not having supervised the agent properly.

A. I only
B. I and II only
C. I, II, and III
D. None of the statements is true.

QUESTION 145

Mr. Noah Scruples is a registered representative with CanDo Broker-Dealers. A client calls and wants Noah to purchase shares of a mutual fund the client has read about. CanDo is not authorized by this particular fund to effect purchases or sales of the fund shares.

Can Noah execute the order anyway?

A. No. This would be considered money laundering, which is highly illegal.
B. No. This is a prohibited practice known as selling away.
C. No. This is a prohibited practice known as front running.
D. Yes. Since this is an unsolicited trade, Noah can execute the transaction on behalf of his client.

QUESTION 146

Noah Scruples, an agent with CanDo Broker-Dealers, just got a copy of the most recent report on a certain stock. The report was generated by CanDo's analyst department and is hot off the presses. It has not yet even been put on the firm's website for the firm's clients.
The analyst department has just changed its recommendation on the stock from "Hold" to "Strong Buy" based on new information that it has obtained on the company.

Can Noah rush to his office to buy shares of the stock before the analysts release their reports to CanDo's clients?

A. Yes. The firm's analysts used publicly available information to assess the stock and make its recommendation, so Noah can buy the stock now on his own account.
B. No. It is unethical for him to trade based on this information before the firm's clients have received the information.
C. No. This is a prohibited activity referred to as "painting the tape."
D. Both B and C are true statements.

QUESTION 147

"T + 3" refers to

A. the form, also known as a "trade ticket," that is filled out when an order is entered into the market.
B. the form that is filled out and sent to the client confirming that the trade has been executed.
C. the fact that the settlement date will be three business days after the trade date, which is the "regular way settlement" for transactions involving stocks and corporate and municipal bonds.
D. a procedure to minimize the potential for money laundering.

QUESTION 148

The C&S Railroad is in the process of issuing new bonds. Before these bonds can be offered for sale,

A. they must be registered with the SEC since railroads are involved in interstate commerce.
B. they must be registered in every state in which the bonds will be sold to investors.
C. they must be registered with the SEC and in each state through which the railroad passes.
D. None of the above statements is true.

ANSWERS

1. **Correct Answer: B**
Explanation: The Uniform Securities Act (USA) provides a model for states to follow when formulating their own securities laws. It does not, itself, contain any laws.

2. **Correct Answer: D**
Explanation: Once you have passed the Series 63 exam, it is the state administrator who can approve or deny your registration. NASAA developed the Uniform Securities Agent State Law Examination and FINRA administers it. The SEC is not a party to the state registration process.

3. **Correct Answer: A**
Explanation: Stocks listed on the Tokyo Stock Exchange would not necessarily be exempt from state registration. Stocks that are registered with the SEC, such as NASDAQ National Market Issue stocks, securities issued or guaranteed by the Canadian government, and securities issued or guaranteed by banks or credit unions are all exempt.

4. **Correct Answer: A**
Explanation: As a director of the firm, Larry would automatically be registered as an investment adviser representative of MoeMoney Investment Advisers. Although directors and officers of the firm are automatically registered as investment adviser representatives, Mary, as a sales representative, would have to apply for her own registration. Curly does not need to be registered since he performs only clerical duties.

5. **Correct Answer: C**
Explanation: Jack will need to register as a sales representative if he participates in the sale of new stock to individual investors. Those who deal directly with the public need to register as sales representatives under the Uniform Securities Act. If Jack limits his involvement to transactions with the underwriters or financial institutions, he need not register.

6. **Correct Answer: A**
Explanation: The main purpose of Blue Sky Laws is to protect individual investors from fraud in their securities market transactions. Requiring the registration of new security issues and the registration of those persons who advise individual investors as well as those involved in the purchase and sale of securities to the public are just some of the regulations designed to do this. There are no provisions designed to protect agents, broker-dealers, or investment advisers and their representatives in any regard.

7. **Correct Answer: C**

Explanation: An individual who represents a broker-dealer in buying and selling securities is called an agent or a registered representative. An agent may also work for an issuer, which refers to the entity that is selling securities to raise money for itself. An underwriter is the entity that aids the issuer in bringing the new securities to market. Administrator is the title many states use to refer to the official in charge of enforcing the state's securities regulations.

8. **Correct Answer: A**

Explanation: The main difference between an agent and a broker-dealer is that an agent represents either a broker-dealer or an issuer and buys and sells securities he doesn't own, receiving a commission for the trades he executes. A broker-dealer, when functioning as a dealer, is buying and selling for his own portfolio, thereby profiting from any price appreciation in the assets in his portfolio.

Both agents and broker-dealers must meet state licensing requirements; both engage in the purchase and sale of stocks, bonds, and option contracts; and both operate in both the primary and secondary markets.

9. Correct Answer: D

Explanation: Rich will not have to register as an investment adviser since he is publishing a legitimate financial newsletter that will be distributed to the general public. The definition of the term "investment adviser" excludes publishers of bona fide business or financial publications that are published regularly and have general circulation.

10. Correct Answer: D

Explanation: Neither SecureMoney Broker-dealers nor Erin must register as an investment adviser based on the facts provided since neither the broker-dealer nor Erin is receiving any compensation for the advice Erin is giving Mrs. McTurk. In this instance, the advice provided is considered incidental to the broker-dealer business.

11. Correct Answer: C

Explanation: Nuering Investment Advisers would not fall under the classification of "institutional investor." Institutional investors are defined as banks, insurance companies, mutual funds, some pension plans, and broker-dealers registered under the Securities Exchange Act of 1934. Investment advisers are not part of this group.

12. Correct Answer: B

Explanation: When Jose buys a 10-year bond that has 6 years remaining to maturity, it is a non-issuer transaction since he is buying it in the secondary market from another investor, and Progress Energy does not benefit from the transaction. If a firm receives money when its securities are sold, it is considered an issuer transaction; otherwise it is a non-issuer transaction. When Progress Energy originally issued the bond, it had ten years to maturity, and Progress Energy received the proceeds from the bond issue; that was an issuer transaction. When Jose buys the bond, another investor is receiving the proceeds. When IBM sells new bonds, regardless of whether it is to the general public or to an institutional investor, IBM receives the proceeds from the transaction, so it is an issuer transaction. Similarly, when a firm that is already publicly held, like Google, sells more shares, the firm receives money from the sale, just as when a firm that is going public for the first time, like NewCorp, receives the proceeds generated through the IPO. Those are examples of issuer transactions.

13. Correct Answer: D

Explanation: The Uniform Securities Act excludes annuity contracts wherein an insurance company promises either to pay a fixed sum, either in a lump amount or through periodic payments, from its definition of a security. Debentures, CDs, and option contracts are all classified as securities under the USA.

14. Correct Answer: C

Explanation: Neither Scenario I nor Scenario IV describes sales as defined by the USA. When an investor receives securities from Company X when Company X merges with a company in which the investor owns stock, Company X is not considered to have sold those securities to the investor. Likewise, when a person uses securities he owns as collateral for a loan, the USA does not consider this to be a sale of the securities.

15. Correct Answer: D

Explanation: Yes. Jeremy is guilty of security violations under the Uniform Securities Act when he provides misleading information when offering securities for sale, even if no securities are actually sold. Partnership interests fall under the definition of securities, and Jeremy's claim to have generated a return of at least 15% on other inventions that he never created is an absolute falsehood.

16. Correct Answer: C

Explanation: An Administrator has broad powers, but he or she cannot deliver a judicial injunction because an Administrator does not have the authority bestowed on a court of law. The Administrator can issue subpoenas to require attendance, participate in evidence gathering, and formulate rules and orders.

17. Correct Answer: A

Explanation: The National Securities Markets Improvement Act of 1996 defined "federal covered securities" and exempted them from state registration requirements. The Gramm-Leach-Bliley Act focused on financial institutions and provided for their registration as broker-dealers under certain conditions. The National Conference of Commissioners on Uniform State Laws (NCCUSL) is the organization that drafted the Uniform Securities Act, which is not comprised of actual laws itself, but is, instead, just a guideline for each state to use when formulating its own securities laws.

18. Correct Answer: D

Explanation: Based on the facts provided, Rich Quick need not register in Florida since he has no offices in the state of Florida, and he is conducting business for existing clients who are merely vacationing in Florida and are not residents of the state.

19. Correct Answer: A

Explanation: Most individual state securities laws continue to be based on the 1956 Uniform Securities Act. Although the Uniform Securities Act was revised in 1985, 1988, and 2002, none of these revisions have been widely incorporated by the individual states. The National Securities Markets Improvement Act of 1996 dealt mainly with the definition of federal covered securities and more efficient management of mutual funds. The focus of the Gramm-Leach-Bliley Act of 1999 was on financial institutions.

20. Correct Answer: B

Explanation: After completing the purchase, BigCash will have to file a new registration application for its new subsidiary, but BigCash can utilize the remainder of any annual filing fees that Target Investments had paid for the year. Although registration applications are never transferable, annual filing fees are.

21. Correct Answer: D

Explanation: In order to maintain its registration with a state, a broker-dealer may be required to take a written or oral exam, pay an annual filing fee, maintain a minimum net capital, and file all advertising material with the state's Administrator. The Administrator of each state has the authority to determine the specific requirements for the state. All of the selections are within the realm of the Administrator's jurisdiction.

22. Correct Answer: A

Explanation: Once a broker-dealer has been granted state registration, that registration is valid until

December 31st of that year. Registration automatically terminates annually on December 31st although an Administrator may elect to revoke or suspend a broker-dealer's registration at any time if the Administrator finds just cause.

23. Correct Answer: A

Explanation: A broker dealer is required to keep his records at least three years.

24. Correct Answer: D

Explanation: Under the guidelines of the USA, none of the entities described in Selections A, B, or C would be required to register with the state as a broker-dealer since the term, as defined by the USA, does not include agents, savings institutions, or entities with no offices in the state who deal exclusively with issuers and/or other broker-dealers, financial institutions, insurance companies, pension funds, or insurance companies. Selections B and C refer to a financial institution and an agent, respectively. In the scenario described in Selection A, the underwriter has no offices in the state and is dealing exclusively with the issuer of the bonds and insurance companies.

25. Correct Answer: C

Explanation: Since Joe Romeo has allowed Betty Buxom to execute trades, a duty that can legally be performed only by a registered broker-dealer or agent, the Administrator may elect to revoke or suspend Joe Romeo's registration, and Joe may also face civil and criminal penalties. Ms. Buxom needed to be registered as an agent prior to effecting any transactions in the securities markets; there is no grace period. The Administrator is not required to take any action, however.

26. Correct Answer: C

Explanation: When Maddie quit her job, her status as a state-registered securities agent was automatically terminated, and she will need to file a new application for registration with the Administrator upon obtaining a position with another broker-dealer. If she does so within thirty days, her registration will become effective as soon as she has filed her application and paid her application fee. While she is required to notify the Administrator that she has terminated her employment with QuikDeals, there is no requirement that she contact any of her clients at QuikDeals.

27. Correct Answer: D

Explanation: Under the guidelines of the USA, when Maddie quits her job as a registered agent with QuikDeals, both QuikDeals and Maddie are responsible for notifying the Administrator. Both the broker-dealer and the agent involved are required to notify the Administrator whenever an agent begins or ends her association with the broker-dealer.

28. Correct Answer: D

Explanation: It depends. Because he is a registered agent in another state and the broker-dealer he is now affiliated with is registered in the state of Massachusetts, Trevor can execute purchases and sales, but only for existing clients while his registration with the Massachusetts Administrator is still pending and only for sixty days. This assumes, of course, Trevor has no violations that would restrict him from registering in Massachusetts.

29. Correct Answer: D

Explanation: Since Ms. Ding is an administrative assistant who is merely providing some information about the fund and is not engaging in the purchase or sale of the fund shares, she does not need to apply for any type of registration. An employee who simply provides price and/or some other pertinent information to the public, but who does not engage in the purchase or sale of securities to the public and does not receive a commission based on the sale of securities is not considered to be an agent or an investment adviser.

30. Correct Answer: C

Explanation: The statement that an agent must demonstrate a specific minimum level of financial stability for his registration application to be accepted is false. The Administrator may require an agent to post a bond, but there are no specific minimum financial requisites that must be met. The Administrator also has the right to terminate an agent's registration if the agent becomes bankrupt. Both the agent and his broker-dealer affiliate are required to inform the Administrator whenever there is a change in the agent's personal information, such as a name change or a change of address.

31. Correct Answer: D

Explanation: Agents, investment advisers, investment adviser representatives, and broker-dealers must all sign a consent to service of process, allowing the Administrator to receive legal documents in their stead. The consent to service of process must accompany the application for registration with the state or the documentation provided with a notice filing when permitted.

32. Correct Answer: D

Explanation: None of the selections describe an "agent," as defined by the Uniform Securities Act (USA.)
Joe is not executing trades for clients of the broker-dealer, and clerical assistants are not classified as agents. Agents must be individuals, so a firm like Freedom broker-dealers would not be considered an agent. A bank is not an individual, and banks are even excluded from the definition of a broker-dealer.

33. Correct Answer: B

Explanation: Investment advisers are required to maintain their records for at least five years.

34. Correct Answer: C

Explanation: Individual states are prohibited from requiring a broker-dealer or investment adviser to file financial reports more frequently than four times a year. Under the Securities and Exchange Act of 1934, individual states are prohibited from imposing more stringent requirements than those already required by the SEC, and the SEC requires quarterly reporting. Therefore, a state may not require that a broker-dealer or investment adviser file monthly reports with it.

35. Correct Answer: C

Explanation: Based on the services A-2-Z provides, it must register with the state as both a broker-dealer and an investment adviser. It is receiving compensation as a broker-dealer for executing purchases and sales of securities for its clients under its basic plan, but it is receiving additional compensation for acting as an investment adviser under the two higher level plans.

36. Correct Answer: D

Explanation: In order for MoeMoney to continue servicing its five individual clients who have relocated to Colorado, neither MoeMoney nor its clients need to do anything. The National Securities Markets Improvement Act of 1996 (NSMIA) established a "deminimis" exemption for investment advisers if they have no office in a state and do business with "no more than five non-institutional clients" during a one-year time frame.

37. Correct Answer: A

Explanation: When Sam and his brother-in-law are caught, Sunny Investment Advisers will not be held liable if it can prove that there was no way it could have or should have known of Sam Shade/Ian Creed's license revocation. The drafters of the Uniform Securities Act were cognizant of the fact that employees can be remarkably deceptive when applying for a position, and because of this the Act indicates that the investment adviser must either "have known or should have known" of the Administrator's adverse decision against the employee in order to itself be deemed liable.

38. Correct Answer: B

Explanation: Regardless of whether the investment adviser is register with the SEC or is itself registered with the state, all of its investment adviser representatives (IARs) are required to register with the state if they operate a place of business in the state.

39. Correct Answer: D

Explanation: A variable annuity is defined as a security, but is exempt from state registration in the opinion of the North American Securities Administrators Association (NASAA.) The Supreme Court of the U.S. passed a ruling that deemed a variable annuity to be a security. The National Securities Market Improvement Act of 1996 (NSMIA) established variable annuities to be federal covered securities, however, since they are, for all intents and purposes, mutual funds. Federal covered securities are exempt from state registration.

40. Correct Answer: C

Explanation: Only Selections II and III are not securities. Neither retirement plans nor commodity futures contracts are deemed to be securities by the Uniform Securities Act. A 401K plan may be invested in securities, but it is not a security itself. A gold futures contract is a contract between two parties for the delivery of the underlying asset, gold. The profits (or losses) are not dependent on the performance of an outside party, which is a critical element, based on a 1946 U.S. Supreme Court decision, which defines a security as "an investment of money. . . with profits to come solely from the efforts of others."

41. Correct Answer: B

Explanation: A viatical settlement is an arrangement under which a terminally ill person sells a second party his life insurance policy at a discount from its face value. When the terminally ill person dies, the buyer of the policy receives its face value. Some states consider viatical settlements to be securities, and they have come under the scrutiny of the NASAA since there is a significant potential for fraud in the writing of these contracts.

42. Correct Answer: A

Explanation: HiGrowth Corporation is the issuer in this instance. Its stock will be sold, and HiGrowth will receive the proceeds from the sale-less BigFee's underwriting spread. Mr. Bigwig is merely HiGrowth's representative in this instance.

43. Correct Answer: C

Explanation: A stock that is listed on the OTC Bulletin Board would not be exempt from state registration unless it already happens to be registered under the Uniform Securities Act. Variable annuities and stocks listed on the American Stock Exchange are classified as federal covered securities by the NSMIA of 1996 and are exempt from state registration. An amendment to the Securities and Exchange Act of 1934 exempts option contracts from state registration.

44. Correct Answer: D

Explanation: The Uniform Securities Act specifies that the initial registration statement should be accompanied by all of the documents listed in the first three selections-a copy of the firm's articles of incorporation and bylaws or their equivalent; copies of any underwriter agreements; and a copy of any indenture that applies to the security being registered. Moreover, these are only some of the documents that need to be included.

45. Correct Answer: C

Explanation: A security's registration is valid for one year after the effective date, which is the date the Administrator approves the registration. If the entire issue has not been sold in this time frame, the offering may be renewed.

46. Correct Answer: B

Explanation: A "notice filing" refers to the filing by a federal covered investment adviser of forms filed with the SEC along with a consent to service of process with the state Administrator. The notice filing must be accompanied by the requisite state filing fee as well.

47. Correct Answer: B

Explanation: Under the 2002 Uniform Securities Act, registration by coordination allows securities that are not federal covered securities to be registered simultaneously with the SEC and with the states in which the securities will be offered for sale. Federal covered securities are exempt from state registration and are required to submit only a notice filing with the Administrator of the state. This is not the same as registration by coordination.

48. Correct Answer: C

Explanation: Newbie may apply for state registration using either the registration by coordination or the registration by qualification method, although the latter method is the most burdensome of the three. The firm is not eligible to register by notification. To be eligible, the offer price of the IPO would have to be at least $5, and the underwriting spread would need to be no greater than 10%.

49. Correct Answer: A

Explanation: The issuer does not have to have both preferred stockholders and common shareholders in order to be eligible for registration by notification. If, however, the issuer does use preferred stock financing, it must not have missed a preferred stock dividend payment.

50. Correct Answer: B

Explanation: Under the registration by coordination process, the security's registration with the state becomes effective immediately after approval by the SEC as long as the registration has been on file for at least 20 days or the Uniform Securities Act has provided an exemption to this waiting period. This assumes, of course, that there is not a stop order or a proceeding pending.

51. Correct Answer: A

Explanation: Registration by exception is not a method that is used to register securities with the state. Registration by notification is a method available for those securities that meet a certain set of criteria and requires the least amount of paperwork. Registration by coordination is the method used for most securities. Registration by qualification is the most burdensome method, requiring a voluminous amount of paperwork.

52. Correct Answer: C

Explanation: Registration by qualification, in its simplest form, requires the issuer to supply voluminous amounts of information about both the firm and its directors, officers, and major shareholders. The state Administrator also has the authority to require even more documentation. It is the least favorite method of registration for obvious reasons.

53. Correct Answer: C

Explanation: The packages are not considered to be securities since each package is simply a purchase and sale agreement between Kevin and another person, with no third party involvement; and since they are not securities, Kevin need not register them with the state. A buyer of one of the packages is not expecting to earn a profit on this investment "solely through the efforts of others," which is one of the defining characteristics of a security, as ruled by the U.S. Supreme Court in 1946.

54. Correct Answer: C

Explanation: The municipal bond issued by the Canadian province of Nova Scotia and the bond issued by Nationwide Insurance Company are both exempt securities under the Uniform Securities Act. Bonds issued by Canadian government entities at both the national and the municipal level and bonds issued by domestic entities in highly regulated industries, as is the case with insurance companies, are exempt. The bond issued by a county in Ireland is not exempt; with the single exception of Canada, only bonds issued by national governments with which the U.S. has diplomatic relations are exempt.

55. Correct Answer: B

Explanation: When Maria purchases shares of Dodge and Cox's International Fund, it is an "issuer" transaction. Shares of mutual funds are bought and sold through the fund itself, so the money she pays for the shares is received by Dodge and Cox, the issuer of the shares. Jacob's purchase of Hasbro stock and Kim's sale of her AT&T bond are non-issuer transactions. Neither Hasbro nor AT&T receive the proceeds from these transactions. In Jacob's case, another investor receives the cash; and in Kim's cash, she receives the cash.

56. Correct Answer: D

Explanation: Under the circumstances described, Fast Eddie can execute the trade for Mr. Moneybags even though SafeAway stock is registered for sale only in the states of Colorado and Wyoming since neither Fast Eddie nor the broker-dealer solicited the transaction, making this an exempt transaction. However, the Massachusetts Administrator may demand that Fast Eddie and his broker-dealer provide proof that the trade was indeed unsolicited.

57. Correct Answer: A

Explanation: Nancy can sell the stock without a problem as executrix of her aunt's estate. This is considered to be a fiduciary transaction and, as such, it is an exempt transaction.

58. Correct Answer: B

Explanation: As defined by the Uniform Securities Act, an exempt security is one that need not be registered in the state in which it is sold. Selections A and D describe exempt transactions. Although securities issued by financial institutions, such as banks, are exempt securities, not all securities that a bank purchases and sells qualify as exempt securities. Private placements may also be exempt transactions, but there are other stipulations that must be met.

59. Correct Answer: D

Explanation: MyTrades falls under the definition of "broker-dealer," as defined by the Uniform Securities Act since Nathan Newmoney is engaged in trading on his own account. The USA defines a broker-dealer as any person that conducts securities transactions on its own account or for others. Both Juan and Michaela are "agents" under the USA definition, and agents are specifically excluded from the definition of a broker-dealer. Marge is also excluded from the definition since she is a loan officer at a bank.

60. Correct Answer: A

Explanation: Keith would not have to register as an agent since he is a salaried employee of a county in Massachusetts selling county-issued bonds to the public. He is not representing a broker-dealer; he is not receiving a commission on the bonds he sells; and he is selling exempt (government-issued) securities. John receives a commission on his sales, so he is considered to be an agent. Stefan is a sales representative employed by a broker-dealer, which makes him an agent under USA guidelines. Even though Preetham is part-owner of the broker-dealer for which he is effecting transactions, he is acting as an agent in doing so.

61. Correct Answer: D

Explanation: When Treadwater Bank and Trust sells municipal bonds it owns to SafeRisk, it does not meet the USA definition of a broker-dealer, an agent, or an issuer. As a bank, Treadwater is automatically excluded as a broker-dealer. Nor can Treadwater be defined as an agent since an agent can only be an individual. Treadwater is not the issuer of the securities; the state and local governments that originally issued the securities are.

62. Correct Answer: C

Explanation: The term "investment adviser" does not apply to Selections II or III. The term "investment adviser" does not apply to a bank or savings institution or to an investment adviser representative. Those persons are specifically excluded from the definition provided by the USA. Any investment advisory firm, regardless of whether it is owned and operated by a sole proprietor, is considered to be an investment adviser. A broker-dealer that charges for its investment advice, even if it claims that the advice is incidental to its business, would be considered an investment adviser due to the special remuneration the firm receives for its advisory services.

63. Correct Answer: C

Explanation: The true statement is C: Investment advisers are required either to be registered with a state or with the SEC, but broker-dealers must be registered with both the SEC and the state. Investment advisers who are federal covered do not need to be registered with the state as well, but they do have to execute a notice filing with the Administrator of any state in which they have an office.

64. Correct Answer: B

Explanation: A sales representative (aka an agent) of a broker-dealer may not make any guarantees. Only three entities are allowed to make guarantees under the Act: Parent companies, which may guarantee the securities of one of its subsidiaries, the U.S. government, and insurance companies.

65. Correct Answer: B

Explanation: An issue of commercial paper with a $100,000 denomination and a maturity of five months with an AA rating from Standard and Poors meets the requirements for an "exempt security." A short-term security, with no more than 270 days to maturity, that has a denomination of at least $50,000, and has a rating of AAA, AA, or A from a recognized rating agency is exempt from registration with the state Administrator.

66. Correct Answer: D

Explanation: Buckeye Investment Advisers is not required to register with the state Administrator since it has no offices in the state and provides portfolio management services to an institutional investor within the state. Both MoeMoney and Financial Freedom must register since they advise more than 5 individual clients. It doesn't matter in that case whether they have offices within the state or not. CanDo is registered only as a broker-dealer, but it has begun offering investment advice for a fee, so it must also register with the state as an investment adviser.

67. Correct Answer: B

Explanation: The state official who has regulatory authority over the securities industry within the state is the administrator.

68. Correct Answer: A

Explanation: The Administrator of a state can gather evidence, but it cannot impose any civil penalties, including the requirement of restitution to victims. These actions can only be performed by a court of law.

69. Correct Answer: C

Explanation: The Administrator can issue an order to cease and desist without providing the party concerned with prior notice. In the cases involving the denial, suspension, or revocation of a license, the Administrator will provide prior notice, along with the opportunity for a hearing, and a written statement of the facts and the legal consequences involved.

70. Correct Answer: C

Explanation: Prior to revoking Samuel's license, the Administrator will provide Samuel with prior notice (I), an opportunity for a hearing (III), and a written statement regarding the facts and the legal consequences (IV).

71. Correct Answer: D

Explanation: Sam has the legitimate option of filing an appeal of the decision in a court of law within 60 days. He will not be able to register as an investment adviser with the SEC or with another state. His application will be denied when it is discovered that Sam has had his license revoked by one state.

72. Correct Answer: B

Explanation: Registration cancellation is a non-punitive order. The Administrator issues a cancellation order if a registered person dies, becomes mentally incompetent, is no longer in business, or is unable to be located.

73. Correct Answer: D

Explanation: Even though Nebulous withdrew its registration from the state, the Administrator has up to a year to take disciplinary action against the broker-dealer if he discovers that Nebulous has been engaged in fraudulent securities transactions after the fact. The Administrator can retroactively begin a revocation or suspension proceeding. Criminal courts can initiate proceedings anytime within five years of the alleged misdeeds.

74. Correct Answer: B

Explanation: Since Wheeler has no offices in the state and is selling bonds from his portfolio to institutional investors, Wheeler need not register in the state, and the securities are exempt from registration. Broker-dealers with no physical location in a state that are doing business with other broker-dealers or with institutional investors such as banks and insurance companies that do have offices in that state are exempted from registering in the state. Securities sales to institutional investors are exempt transactions, and securities sold in exempt transactions are themselves exempt from state registration requirements.

75. Correct Answer: A

Explanation: As an employee of Giant Investment Advisers who provides investment advice to clients, Jack Bean is an investment adviser representative. Giant is the investment adviser. Agents are employed by broker-dealers.

76. Correct Answer: B

Explanation: As an employee of Spyder Broker-Dealers who executes trades for clients, Ms. Muffet is an agent who works for the broker-dealer Spyder. She does not provide investment advice for a fee, so she is neither an investment adviser nor an investment adviser representative.

77. Correct Answer: C

Explanation: The criminal penalties specified by the Uniform Securities Act for "willful violations" of the act are up to 3 years in prison or a $5,000 fine, or both, for each violation.

78. Correct Answer: C

Explanation: Yes. The investors have a civil claim against George under the Uniform Securities Act and can sue for the return of their original investment, plus interest, reasonable attorneys' fees, and court costs. There is no provision for pain and suffering. Partnership interests fall under the definition of securities, so the Uniform Securities Act does apply, and George sold the interests illegally. As securities, they were required to be registered with the state before they could be sold.

79. Correct Answer: D

Explanation: Yes, there have been violations of securities laws in this instance; the promissory note required registration, and Ms. Naiveté has been defrauded. Promissory notes are considered to be securities as defined by the Uniform Securities Act and, as such, must be registered with the state before they can be offered for sale. Furthermore, a promissory note is a promise to repay, and Mr. Smooth has defaulted on this promise after telling Ms. Naiveté that the investment was close to being risk-free. In essence, he took Ms. Naiveté's money under false pretenses when he sold her the note, and that is the definition of fraud.

80. Correct Answer: C

Explanation: If you discover that a security you purchased has not been registered with the state and was sold unlawfully, you can file a civil claim against the seller as long as you do so within two years from discovery or three years from the event, whichever comes first, under the guidelines of the Uniform Securities Act.

Therefore, if you know about an unlawful sale for more than two years or if the sale took place more than three years ago, you cannot sue. The statute of limitations has expired.

81. Correct Answer: A

Explanation: Since Iggy realized the promissory note he had sold to the investor required state registration and sent a formal offer of rescission to the investor, he cannot be sued for civil damages if the investor has not responded to the offer within 30 days. The investor has 30 days to accept or reject the offer. If he either rejects it or fails to accept it by not responding to the offer at all, the investor has lost the right to sue for damages.

82. Correct Answer: D

Explanation: If Arnold loses his money because he took the advice of his investment adviser and reallocated a large percentage of his money from bonds to an aggressive growth mutual fund, he can sue the investment adviser in civil court for the amount of his losses, plus interest, court costs, and attorneys' fees. The courts do not award damages for "pain and suffering" in these cases. The investment adviser failed in his fiduciary responsibility to Arnold in recommending that a 74-year old man reallocate a large percentage of his money from the relative safety of bonds to the much riskier investment of an aggressive growth mutual fund.

83. Correct Answer: C

Explanation: Yes. Julia has violated a provision of the Uniform Securities Act by distributing business cards that indicate she is a "state-registered" investment adviser because she has not yet received notification of the acceptance of her application by the state Administrator. The filing of an application for registration is not the same as registration, and the placement of the cards is, at this early point, false advertising.

84. Correct Answer: D

Explanation: Yes, Ari will be violating a securities law if he distributes the business cards because the cards suggest he has been approved by the state Administrator. The Uniform Securities Act specifically states that the effective registration of a person does not mean that the Administrator has "given approval to" that person. Any statement to this effect is considered an unlawful representation.

85. Correct Answer: A

Explanation: An Administrator may not deny, suspend, or revoke the license of a person simply because the applicant has never before worked in the securities industry if that person has received the training necessary. The Uniform Securities Act specifically states that the order cannot be entered ". . .solely on the basis of lack of experience if the applicant or registrant is qualified by training, knowledge, or both."

86. Correct Answer: C

Explanation: If a person has appropriately and truthfully disclosed every material fact on its application for registration, the Administrator has 90 days after the registration becomes effective to commence a proceeding to deny, suspend, or revoke the license. If the Administrator has known about the fact for longer than this, he may not begin a proceeding against that person according to the Uniform Securities Act.

87. Correct Answer: D

Explanation: A broker-dealer can be a partnership, an individual, or a sole-proprietorship under the guidelines of the Uniform Security Act.

88. Correct Answer: C

Explanation: If Harry Lange is managing the investment portfolio of Fidelity Magellan Mutual Fund, he is an investment adviser. He is making the investment decisions and receives a percentage of the assets under management as his compensation. He is not selling the mutual fund or the fund's investors anything, which is the job of a broker-dealer or an agent. Fidelity Magellan is the investment company.

89. Correct Answer: C

Explanation: An investment adviser provides investment advice to clients and may also buy and sell securities in their clients' accounts for the clients. He does not, however, sell securities to his clients.

90. Correct Answer: A

Explanation: When applying for registration as an agent, you will need to submit a U-4. No photograph is necessary. Form ADV is used to register as an investment adviser, and only broker-dealers and investment advisers must meet the state's minimum net capital requirement.

91. Correct Answer: A

Explanation: If Bootstraps hires three individuals to sell promissory notes to the public, both the notes and the three individuals hired to sell the notes must be registered with the state. The promissory notes are securities and, therefore, are required to be registered with the state before they can be offered for sale. The three individuals are working for the issuer, Bootstraps, to sell its securities to the public. This makes them agents, according to the Uniform Securities Act, and they must be registered as agents with the state.

92. Correct Answer: D

Explanation: When Skip leaves one broker-dealer and signs on with another, all three entities-Skip, Mars, and Venus-must report this to the state Administrator. Under the Uniform Securities Act, when an agent leaves a broker-dealer, both the agent and the broker-dealer are required to report this to the state Administrator, and when an agent begins employment with a new broker-dealer, both the agent and the new broker-dealer must report it.

93. Correct Answer: C

Explanation: When the net worth of a broker-dealer falls below the minimum net capital requirement specified by the state, the broker-dealer must notify the Administrator of this fact by the close of business on the next business day according to the Uniform Securities Act.

94. Correct Answer: C

Explanation: Barring no irregularities, after you have filed for registration as an agent, you should receive your license within 30 days. More specifically, your license will be approved "no later than noon of the 30th day after filing."

95. Correct Answer: B

Explanation: Since S. White is already registered in the state of Kentucky and meeting the net capital requirement of that state, the Investment Advisers Act of 1940 stipulates that Virginia cannot require a higher minimum net capital. The Act states that if an investment adviser is registered in one state and is meeting its net capital requirement, a second state cannot impose a higher net capital requirement on the investment adviser.

96. Correct Answer: B

Explanation: "A state cannot require a higher minimum net capital for investment advisers than the amount specified by the Investment Advisers Act of 1940" is a false statement. The Investment Advisers Act of 1940 does not specify a minimum net capital requirement. The Act simply indicates that if an investment adviser is already registered in one state and meeting that state's minimum net capital requirement, a second state can't impose a higher net capital requirement on it.

97. Correct Answer: B

Explanation: Only selections I and III are subject to post-registration provisions. Broker-dealers and investment advisers can be required to file advertising materials and financial reports with the Administrator, as specified by the Administrator. They are also required to keep records to the specifications of the Administrator.

These records will include items such as client e-mails, client letters of complaint, and advertising brochures and must be kept for three years.

98. Correct Answer: C

Explanation: Even after Fly-By-Night has closed its doors, it is required to preserve and maintain all records, including client transactions and communications, advertising materials, and the financial statements of the business for five years, under the guidelines of the Uniform Securities Act.

99. Correct Answer: D

Explanation: Once you have passed the necessary exams and are applying for registration as an agent, you must pay the full annual fee and your license will expire on December 31st of the current year, no matter how late in the year it is.

100. Correct Answer: C

Explanation: To continue operating as an agent, broker-dealer, investment adviser, or investment adviser representative next year, you must pay your filing fee to renew your license by December 31st of this year. Otherwise, your license will expire. There is no grace period.

101. Correct Answer: C

Explanation: BigFee Investment Bankers is acting as a dealer. In underwriting the securities, the firm is purchasing them from HiGrowth and selling the securities to the public. If the securities don't sell for the amount that BigFee thinks they can, BigFee takes the loss as owner of the securities.

102. Correct Answer: D

Explanation: GetErDone Broker-Dealers is the broker in this scenario. GetErDone is simply finding buyers for the securities and receives a commission for doing so. GetErDone is not itself purchasing the securities in the scenario described. It would be considered unethical for the broker-dealer to do so since they are required to make a bona fide public offering of all of the securities allotted to them for distribution under NASAA Model Rules.

103. Correct Answer: B

Explanation: When a bond issue has been effectively registered with the state Administrator, it can be offered for sale in the state. The bond's acceptance by the Administrator simply means that the issuer has supplied enough information in order for an investor to judge the quality of the bond for himself; it in no way implies that the bond is of sound quality. It could, in fact, be a very risky security and still have met the registration requirements.

104. Correct Answer: B

Explanation: BondsRUs is guilty of overcharging its clients by unreasonable markups. A $9 dealer's spread on a risk-free investment such as a Treasury bond is unwarranted, and this practice is prohibited.

Based on the information provided, BondsRUs is not guilty of fraud since it appears that the firm is revealing the markup in its confirmation statements. The clients just aren't paying attention.

105. Correct Answer: D

Explanation: A broker-dealer of commodity futures contracts is guilty of nothing under the Uniform Securities Act since a commodity futures contract is not a security as defined by the USA. The broker-dealer may, however, find himself in trouble with the Commodity Futures Trading Commission, which is the regulatory agency of the futures market.

106. Correct Answer: D

Explanation: Turnover is guilty of nothing when it hires 50 new employees, but doesn't include this information in its prospectus because this is not a material fact. Most of the employees have been hired to replace middle-level managers who have retired, and these employees wouldn't be considered significant enough to affect the price of the stock in any way. If Turnover had hired a new CEO, that would be a material fact that must be disclosed.

107. Correct Answer: C

Explanation: Yes. YourMoney is guilty of fraud in its claim that "an investor can expect the fund to continue earning a return higher than the S&P 500 Index." Past performance is no indication of future performance, and this statement is clearly a misstatement of a material fact. In fact, because the securities the fund invests in are riskier than average, the fund returns can be expected to fall harder than the S&P 500 Index in a market downturn.

108. Correct Answer: A

Explanation: Yes. Constance is guilty of fraud. She misled her client into thinking he couldn't lose money if he invested the money in a U.S. government bond fund. Although U.S. government bonds are referred to as risk-free, this just means they are considered free from default risk. The value of the bonds-and, therefore, the

U.S. government bond funds-will change with changes in interest rates. As an investment adviser representative, Constance should know this. Regardless of whether or not she does, she is guilty of fraud simply by providing the misleading information. If she knew it and deliberately misled the client, she is guilty of criminal fraud.

109. Correct Answer: C

Explanation: Yes. The broker-dealer is making a misleading statement in an advertising brochure in order to convince investors to do business with the firm. This is deceitful and misleading, and persons involved in the securities industry are prohibited from making deceitful and misleading statements.

110. Correct Answer: C

Explanation: Selections I, II, and IV are correct. An investment adviser is permitted to be compensated with a share of the capital gains of the client's portfolio if the client is a mutual fund, a credit union, or a private client with at least $750,000 invested through the investment adviser. More generally, the adviser can charge a fee based on the capital appreciation of the portfolio if the client is an institutional investor, a private client with a net worth of at least $1.5 million, or a private client with at least $750,000 invested with the investment adviser.

111.   Correct Answer: C

Explanation: Only Selections I and III are correct. If one of the partners dies, Alter Advisers must inform both the state Administrator and the firm's clients of this event. This represents a change in the partnership. The SEC need not be notified since Alter Advisers is not registered with the SEC.

112.   Correct Answer: B

Explanation: Only Selections I and II are true. Switch must obtain the approval of its clients before the partners can sell their interests, and Switch must notify the state Administrator of this event. Whenever a change in partnership will result in new ownership of the business, which is the case when an external entity acquires a 60% interest, an investment adviser must get its clients' approval. As a state-registered investment adviser, switch also needs to notify the state Administrator.
The SEC does not require notification since Switch is not a federal covered investment adviser.

113.   Correct Answer: C

Explanation: Yes. Noah is guilty of not following a client's instructions and could have his license revoked. A refusal to act on a client's legitimate order is a prohibited practice, even if the client would have lost money after-the-fact.

114.   Correct Answer: C

Explanation: Yes. In recommending that Mr. and Mrs. Cleaver and their son allocate their assets in identical fashions, Mr. Eddie has made an unsuitable recommendation since investors with different investment time horizons have different investment needs. Making unsuitable recommendations is a prohibited practice, and Mr. Eddie could have his license suspended or revoked.

115.   Correct Answer: C

Explanation: Yes. When Stu recommends an investment in municipal bonds for a classic IRA account, he has made an unsuitable recommendation, which is a prohibited practice, and he can have his license revoked or suspended. Municipal bonds are not suitable investments for a classic IRA because municipal bonds pay interest that is at least free from federal taxation, so they offer a lower yield than fully taxable bonds of similar risk. The money in a classic IRA grows tax-free anyway, so the client is getting a lower yield with no benefit.

116.   Correct Answer: A

Explanation: Yes. If Ken is getting up each morning in order to collect news that he can use to pressure his clients to buy and sell their securities, Ken is engaging in churning and can have his license revoked or suspended for this prohibited practice. A lot of the news might have a short-term effect on a particular industry, but any profits gained by trying to time the market will often not be sufficient to cover the commissions that the investor had to pay on the transactions and the taxes they may have to pay on the short-term capital gains they realized when they sold securities. Regardless, it doesn't matter whether his clients' accounts show a profit or not.

117.   Correct Answer: B

Explanation: No, you cannot execute this transaction unless you and your broker-dealer have a written document that gives Mr. Sailor's son the power-of-attorney to trade on his account. Otherwise, you will be executing an order from an unauthorized third party, which is a prohibited practice, and you can lose your license for doing so.

118.   Correct Answer: C

Explanation: Given that you have advised Mr. Crochety that this is not a wise move and he still insists on it, you should protect yourself by getting it in writing. In no case, however, can you require a client to sign an affidavit of liability waver, nor can you refuse to follow his adamant instructions.

119.   Correct Answer: D

Explanation: There is no specified turnover ratio assigned to the prohibited practice of churning since some investors are simply more frequent traders than others.

120.   Correct Answer: A

Explanation: In recommending that Annie buy stock in Alcon because its stock is guaranteed to pay a dividend of $2.21 a share or higher, Goldie has committed fraud. The company itself could not even make such a guarantee legitimately. Goldie may also be guilty of an unsuitable recommendation since factors other than dividend yield-such as the risk of the investment--should have been considered. That being said, Goldie is permitted to make recommendations for specific investments as an agent of a broker-dealer, as long as she doesn't receive special compensation for it.

121.   Correct Answer: C

Explanation: No, Mr. Ranger has not violated any laws or engaged in any prohibited practices in his recommendation to Mr. Tonto. He has simply informed Mr. Tonto of the rumor and has told him of the risk involved, and he has not lied or misled Mr. Tonto about the investment. He is also well aware of his friend's risk tolerance level, so he is not making an unsuitable recommendation. This is not considered insider trading since there is no way Mr. Ranger can know whether or not the rumor is true. Selection A is not true because there can be violations of laws or practices, even if the agent and client are friends.

122.   Correct Answer: C

Explanation: No, Joe cannot take his client's offer of a loan because it could lead to a conflict of interest--if not today, perhaps in the future--and as a fiduciary Joe will be expected to put this client's welfare ahead of his own. If it takes him a lot longer than expected to get on his feet again, he may be tempted to act in his own best interest.

123.   Correct Answer: B

Explanation: An agent selling a Massachusetts general obligation bond can legitimately tell the investor that the interest income he receives from the bond will be free from federal taxation. It is not, however, a risk-free investment. States may default on their bond issues, and bonds issued by states are not guaranteed by the federal government.

124.   Correct Answer: A

Explanation: Mr. Hill has made an unsuitable recommendation in recommending a 60% investment in bonds to clients in their mid-20s with an investment goal of early retirement, and his license can be suspended or revoked because of this. Bonds do not generate the returns that stocks do, and Jack and Jill are unlikely to be able to retire by the time they are 50 with such a high percentage invested in bonds. Given their investment time horizon, they can invest in growth and aggressive growth stocks, which offer significantly higher returns and will advance them toward their goal, since they can ride the waves of the up and down markets. This, of course, assumes that they are risk-tolerant enough to do so. There has been no fraud since a couple in their mid-20s can retire by the time they turn 50 if they have reasonably well-paying jobs, are frugal, and invest wisely.

125.   Correct Answer: A

Explanation: Finn has not violated any laws or engaged in any prohibited practices in using the words "Certified Financial Planner" on his business cards. Had he indicated he had been certified or approved by the state, he would have been in violation, but he is allowed to indicate a certification with a professional organization in any advertising literature.

126.   Correct Answer: D

Explanation: After attending the ARP seminars on asset allocation for senior citizens, Elizabeth and her team cannot represent themselves as certified senior citizen investment advisers, print "Senior-Citizen Investment Specialists" on their business cards, or indicate that they are certified by the ARP program. Under the NASAA model rules, their attendance does not entitle them to say they are in any way especially certified to serve senior citizens. The attendance certification they received does not have any competency requirements attached.

127.   Correct Answer: D

Explanation: Ms. Swyne must provide Bear Broker-Dealers with a copy of the complaint sent by Mr. Wolf. Bear Broker-Dealers is required to respond to this complaint in writing and keep a record of it. E-mails are treated the same as snail-mails.

128.   Correct Answer: D

Explanation: Only selections II and III are violations of insider trading rules. If you receive an unsolicited call from a client requesting a sale (or purchase) of that firm's stock, it is not considered to be an insider transaction. If you have insider information from you brother about the merger of VideoMagic with another firm, you cannot buy stock yourself in the target firm in anticipation of a rise in price, nor can you recommend the stock to customers based on your expectation of a stock price increase.

129.   Correct Answer: D

Explanation: Both statements A and B are true. As an agent for broker-dealer CanDo, Mr. Teche is required to inform CanDo in writing before accepting any outside position that will provide him with additional compensation, and CanDo has the right to deny Mr. Teche the permission to accept this position.

130.   Correct Answer: B
Explanation: A deferred annuity would be an unsuitable recommendation for your 68-year-old client. These annuities charge significant penalties for early withdrawals-and "early" can mean before 10 years, or even longer. A 68-year-old client may have the need to withdraw his money early to make medical payments.

131.   Correct Answer: A

Explanation: When Sly has his client pay for a stock purchase by making the check out to Sly himself, he has engaged in the prohibited practice of commingling. Ms. Fox is also engaged in a prohibited practice, but she is engaged in making unauthorized transactions. Mr. Hawk is doing nothing wrong. It is typical for clients to leave securities on deposit with their broker-dealers in what is called "street name." This makes it easier for the client to sell the securities later on since he physically will not have to deliver the securities to the broker, for one thing.

132.   Correct Answer: C

Explanation: It may be permissible for you and your brother to open a joint account to invest in this partnership since he is a family member, but it will require the written consent of both your brother and your firm, and your firm is under no obligation to give its consent.

133.   Correct Answer: D

Explanation: Yes. You are guilty of illegal insider trading because you traded on information that was not yet public. Your neighbor and her brother did not execute any trades based on the information, so they're innocent, as is the agent who executed your purchase order, who had no way of knowing that you had insider knowledge when you placed the order.

134.   Correct Answer: C

Explanation: If Mr. Pulse wants you to place an order to buy a firm that he thinks will become a target of Microsoft based on seeing Bill Gates and the owner of the firm dining together, you should, as his adviser, inform him that he may be jumping the gun and drawing a false conclusion, but you should place the order if he continues to insist. It is a legitimate order, and you are obligated to follow his instructions. It does not constitute illegal insider trading because Mr. Pulse has no way of knowing what the two men were talking about. They may just be old high school buddies catching up on the news.

135.   Correct Answer: A

Explanation: Mina should have notified SecureMoney in writing before taking on the job at the fitness club. Regardless of whether the job has anything to do with finance, an agent must notify her broker-dealer in writing prior to engaging in any extracurricular activity for which she gets paid. She is not required to send any notice to the Administrator, however.

136.   Correct Answer: D

Explanation: The agent's commission does not appear on an order ticket. It does appear on the trade confirmation, however, which the client receives.

137.   Correct Answer: B

Explanation: If Rich Quick is able to earn profits 95% of the time by trading on abnormalities he observes in bond yield spreads, he is skilled. There is nothing illegal in what he is doing. Arbitrageurs attempt to earn profits when they observe what they believe to be mispriced securities, and this is an accepted activity. Rich is not using insider information; bond yields are publicly available information.

138.   Correct Answer: D

Explanation: All of the items listed appear on a trade confirmation-the client's account number, the commission, and the settlement date-as well as a lot of additional information.

139.   Correct Answer: B

Explanation: Trade confirmations must be received by the customer no later than the settlement date.

140. **Correct Answer: B**

Explanation: The settlement date is the date that the buyer must pay for the securities purchased. For stocks and bonds other than U.S. Treasury securities, this date is the third business day after the trade. For U.S. Treasuries and options that sell on exchanges, the settlement date is the next business day.

141. **Correct Answer: A**

Explanation: If Alice places a market order to buy call options on Tuesday, August 10th, she will have to pay for them on Wednesday, August 11th, the next business day. Options and U.S. government bonds settle on the day after the trade date, or T + 1.

142. **Correct Answer: A**

Explanation: If your client places an order to purchase 500 shares of Oracle on the open market on Wednesday, September 15th, payment will be due on Monday, September 20th. The settlement date for stock transactions is T + 3, which means the third business day after the trade. Saturday is not a business day.

143. **Correct Answer: D**

Explanation: If you execute a stock transaction for a client on Thursday, September 23rd, the settlement date for that trade will be Tuesday, September 28th, which is T + 3, meaning three business days after the trade date.

144. **Correct Answer: D**

Explanation: If the CFO called his broker and sold some of the shares he owns today, none of the statements is true. Insider trading is only illegal if the insider trades on information that the public does not yet have. In this case, the information has already been made publicly available, so no one has done anything illegal. Insiders to the company are allowed to buy and sell shares of their firm's stock as long as they are not acting on private information.

145. **Correct Answer: B**

Explanation: No. If CanDo is not authorized to effect purchases and sales of the fund, Noah would be engaged in the prohibited practice known as selling away if he were to execute the order. If his broker-dealer is not authorized to trade a security, Noah can't either.

146. **Correct Answer: B**

Explanation: No. It is unethical for him to trade based on the information that just came from the analysts before the firm's clients have the information. This is a prohibited practice called "front running."

147. **Correct Answer: C**

Explanation: "T + 3" is an abbreviation indicating that the settlement date will be three business days after the trade date, which is the "regular way settlement" for transactions involving stocks and corporate and municipal bonds.

148. **Correct Answer: D**

Explanation: None of the statements is true because securities issued by highly regulated industries, such as the railroad industry are exempt from registration with both the SEC and the states.